The
HIDDEN PLACES
of
THE THAMES VALLEY

Edited by
Joanna Billing

© Travel Publishing Ltd. 1999

Published by:
Travel Publishing Ltd
7a Apollo House, Calleva Park
Aldermaston, Berks, RG7 8TN

ISBN 1-902-00734-4

© Travel Publishing Ltd 1999

First Published:	*1991*	*Fourth Edition:*	*1999*
Second Edition:	*1993*		
Third Edition:	*1997*		

Regional Titles in the Hidden Places Series:

Cambridgeshire & Lincolnshire	Channel Islands
Cheshire	Chilterns
Cornwall	Devon
Dorset, Hants & Isle of Wight	Essex
Gloucestershire	Heart of England
Hereford, Worcs & Shropshire	Highlands & Islands
Kent	Lake District & Cumbria
Lancashire	Norfolk
Northeast Yorkshire	Northumberland & Durham
North Wales	Nottinghamshire
Peak District	Potteries
Somerset	South Wales
Suffolk	Surrey
Sussex	Thames Valley
Warwickshire & W Midlands	Wiltshire
Yorkshire Dales	

National Titles in the Hidden Places Series:

England	Ireland
Scotland	Wales

Printing by: Ashford Press, Gosport
Maps by: © MAPS IN MINUTES ™ (1998)
Line Drawings: Dawn Paynter
Editor: Joanna Billing
Cover Design: Lines & Words, Aldermaston
Cover Photographs: Sonning Lock, Sonning, Berkshire; Old Stocks, Woodstock, Oxfordshire; The Church, Cookham, Berkshire. © Britain on View/Stockwave.

FOREWORD

The Hidden Places series is a collection of easy to use travel guides taking you, in this instance, on a relaxed but informative tour of the Thames Valley, which wends its way through the varied landscape of Berkshire and Oxfordshire. Berkshire is a county offering the visitor rolling downland and tiny picturesque villages in the west and a combination of unspoilt countryside and historic towns by the Thames in the east. Oxfordshire is famous for its medieval capital city of *"dreaming spires"* but possesses a rich diversity of scenery, history and architecture from the edge of the Cotswolds in the west, through the long rich reaches of the Thames to the sweeping downlands in the east.

Our books contain a wealth of interesting information on the history, the countryside, the towns and villages and the more established places of interest in the counties. But they also promote the more secluded and little known visitor attractions and places to stay, eat and drink many of which are easy to miss unless you know exactly where you are going.

We include hotels, inns, restaurants, public houses, teashops, various types of accommodation, historic houses, museums, gardens, garden centres, craft centres and many other attractions throughout the Thames Valley, all of which are comprehensively indexed. Most places have an attractive line drawing and are cross-referenced to coloured maps found at the rear of the book. We do not award merit marks or rankings but concentrate on describing the more interesting, unusual or unique features of each place with the aim of making the reader's stay in the local area an enjoyable and stimulating experience.

Whether you are visiting the area for business or pleasure or in fact are living in the counties we do hope that you enjoy reading and using this book. We are always interested in what readers think of places covered (or not covered) in our guides so please do not hesitate to use the reader reaction forms provided to give us your considered comments. We also welcome any general comments which will help us improve the guides themselves. Finally if you are planning to visit any other corner of the British Isles we would like to refer you to the list of other *Hidden Places* titles to be found at the rear of the book.

CONTENTS

West Berkshire

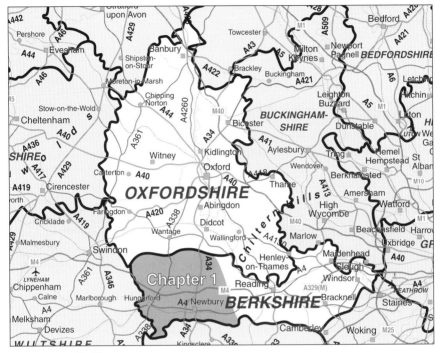

This western area of Berkshire is dominated by the old Cloth Town of Newbury which today is perhaps better known for its first class race course. The training of race horses is also a serious pursuit in the region and the villages of Lambourn and East Ilsley are famous for the horses they have produced which are trained on the undulating downlands which run along the northern county border.

Another feature of West Berkshire are the communication routes which flow across the region linking London with the West Country. Dominated today by the M4 motorway, the ancient Ridgeway path, England's oldest road, follows the county border with Oxfordshire. Thought to have become a route in the Bronze Age, over the centuries many different people have used the trackway as a thoroughfare for trade with the remoter parts of southwest England.

Completed in 1810, the Kennet and Avon Canal crosses southern England from Bristol to join the River Thames at Reading. Entering the county at

Hungerford, this major waterway passes through a charming rural landscape as it winds through villages and market towns. The canal prospered until the arrival of the Great Western Railway in 1841 and by the 1950s it was largely unnavigable. Fortunately, after a full clearing and restoration programme, the canal can once again by travelled its full length and it provides a wide variety of leisure activities for all.

LAMBOURN

Lying up on the Berkshire Downs, in the extreme west of the county, this village, which has the feel of a small town, is well known for the race horses that are trained here. Once known as Chipping - which means market - Lambourn, the village once had not only a weekly market but also three annual fairs.

Whether a horse racing fan or not, Lambourn has plenty to amuse and occupy the visitor. Its medieval **Church of St Michael** is one of the finest parish churches in Berkshire. Originally Norman and constructed on the cruciform plan, over the years the church has been greatly altered and extended though the west end still has its Norman doorway, complete with zigzag ornamentation. Close to the church can be found the pleasing **Isbury Almshouses**, built around a quadrangle, that were founded in 1502 though the present houses date from 1852.

The **Lambourn Trainers' Association** organise guided tours of the village's famous stables and also the trips up to the gallops to view the horses going through their paces. An informative and enjoyable way to spent a couple of hours, the visits, for obvious reasons, have to be by appointment only.

To the north of the village are **Lambourn Seven Barrows**, one of the most impressive Bronze Age burial sites in the country. However, the name is somewhat misleading as there are no fewer than 32 barrows up here but arguably the best group consists of six bowl barrows, two double bowl barrows, two saucer barrows, and a single disc barrow.

Found in the heart of this ancient village that has long been associated with the horse racing industry lies the part Tudor-part Georgian home of Jackie Warr, **The Downs House**. As its age would suggest, this house has plenty of character and, as Jackie has lived here since the 1960s, not only is it a true home but this kind and warm hostess also has a great knowledge of the local area. Offering bed and breakfast accommodation in three delightful en-suite guest rooms, The Downs House is an excellent place to stay for those interested in finding out about beautiful and historic area. Guests are not only treated to a delicious homecooked breakfast each morning but, by prior arrangement, Jackie also provides evening meals that include a selection of vegetarian options. A superb place for children, one of the rooms is a comfortable family room with plenty of space for two youngsters, Jackie is very happy to help point guests in the right

**The Downs House, 32 Lambourn High Street, Lambourn,
Berks RG17 8XN Tel: 01488 71637**

direction for Lambourn's famous horse training stables and exercise grounds but she is also delighted to assist guests in following more unusual pursuits and interests in the area.

AROUND LAMBOURN

FAWLEY   MAP 1 REF C8
4 miles NE of Lambourn off the A338

This small downlands village is known to many avid Thomas Hardy readers as the village of Marygreen in one of his most tragic novels, *Jude the Obscure*. The writer's grandmother, Mary Hardy, is known to have lived here with her aunt for the first 13 years of her life following the death of both her parents. Though Mary never spoke of her painful memories, her sad early life was known to Hardy and they certainly coloured his view of the village. The ill-fated hero of the book, Jude Fawley, is said to have been very much based on Hardy himself and, when the writer visited the village to trace his relatives, he wrote in his journal "I entered a ploughed field which might have been called the Valley of Brown Melancholy, where the silence was remarkable."

FARNBOROUGH
MAP 1 REF C8

6½ miles NE of Lambourn off the B4494

Found high on the north Berkshire chalklands, this village was home, for a time, to the poet John Betjeman. In the parish church, with its fine 15th-century tower, can be seen a memorial window to the village's most famous resident that was created by John Piper.

EAST ILSLEY
MAP 1 REF D8

10 miles E of Lambourn off the A34

This attractive downland village has managed to retain several interesting features and, in particular, by the village pond can be seen the winding mechanism of the now long disused village well. However, it is on sheep that the village prospered and from the beginning of the 17th century East Ilsley held fortnightly sheep fairs that were second only in size to Smithfield, London. At their peak in the 19th century, permanent pens were erected in the main street to contain the animals and, on one day, it was recorded that 80,000 sheep were penned.

There is an old jingle about the village which goes: "Far famed for sheep and wool, though not for spinners, for sportsmen, doctors, publicans, and sinners." Naturally, whilst the sheep fairs were flourishing, the publicans were also mak-

Village Green and Duck Pond, East Ilsley

ing good money but after the last fair, in 1934, the number of inns fell from as many as 26, at one time, to just three.

Today, along with its neighbour, West Ilsley, the village is associated with race horses which use the gallops on the downs as their training grounds. Though not as large as Lambourn, there are still successful stables in the area.

COMPTON   MAP 1 REF D9
11½ miles E of Lambourn off the A34

The origins of this ancient village stretch back beyond the time of the Norman Conquest and into prehistoric times. About a mile south of the village lie the remains of an Iron Age hill fort, **Perborough Castle**, which is thought to be one of a series of hill forts that lay close to the Ridgeway. To the northeast of the village, just above the Ridgeway, lies **Lowbury Hill**. Here can be seen the remains of a Roman temple, another example of early inhabitants of the area, on the hill's summit along with a Roman military outpost.

By the time of the Domesday Survey, in 1086, Compton was a well established settlement with two manors, both of which fell into the hands of supporters of William the Conqueror. Over the years, the manor came into the possession of the Lloyd family and the lands and farms were later sold off to the sitting tenants.

During the 19th century, as the railway track was laid from Newbury to the Great Western Railway depot at Didcot, Compton Station became an important centre for the passage of sheep to and from the great East Ilsley fairs. Pens were erected in the station's sidings to contain the animals waiting to be transported. However, in the 1960s, the decline in the wool trade became so acute that the station was forced to close.

HAMPSTEAD NORREYS   MAP 1 REF D9
12 miles E of Lambourn on the B4009

Just to the north of the village lies **Wyld Court Rainforest**, a fascinating conservation centre that is owned by the World Land Trust. The Trust, a charitable organisation founded in 1989, not only purchases and protects areas of tropical forests all over the world but also concerns itself with education. Here, at the indoor rainforest, where the temperature never falls below 70°C, visitors have the opportunity to walk through the humid and shadowy jungles of the Lowland Tropical Forests, the cool, orchid-festooned and ferny Cloudforests, and the Amazon with its amazing flowers and wonderful bromeliads. There is also a unique collection of spectacular and rare plants, tranquil pools, the sounds of the topics, and rainforest animals including a pair of time marmosets, tree frogs, iguanas, and Courtney, the dwarf crocodile.

BEEDON
MAP 1 REF D9
10 miles E of Lambourn off the A34

Found to the northwest, and just the other side of the main A34, is the tiny village of Beedon. Beginning life as a beerhouse on the busy Newbury to Oxford turnpike road, the charming early 18th-century **Coach and Horses** inn remains an attractive stopping place for travellers who find themselves in this now quiet backwater. Managed since 1997 by Pat and Tony Holman, a friendly couple who are also members of the British Institute of Inn Keeping, this delightful village pub welcomes all who venture through the doors. Warm and cosy inside, customers are met with roaring log fires in winter, soft lighting in

**The Coach and Horses, Worlds End, Beedon, near Newbury,
Berks RG20 8SE Tel: 01635 248743**

the lounge bar, a vast array of brass plates and ornaments, and a mass of pictures on the walls that are all the work of local artists.

As well as serving a range of traditional real ales and beers, there is also an extensive menu of homecooked fare - all freshly prepared by Pat - served at both lunchtime and in the evening (except Tuesday lunches and Sunday evenings) that is sure to tempt all the family. A relaxed and leisurely pace ensures that everyone can enjoy their meal and drink in peace and, during the summer, not only is there an attractive garden but also swings and a play area for the children.

LECKHAMPSTEAD
MAP 1 REF C9
8 miles SE of Lambourn off the B4494

The name of this charming little village describes a farm having a kitchen garden and it is derived from the Anglo Saxon word *'leac'*. Well established by the time of the Domesday Book, in which it is mentioned, Leckhampstead has, on its triangular village green, an unusual **war memorial**. Comprising an obelisk placed on a plinth, there are two clock faces (one facing north, the other south which incorporate various different types of ammunition in them) above the names of the dead of the parish. The theme continues as the chains surrounding the monument have come from a battleship that took part in the battle of Jutland and they are supported on spent shell cases.

The village is also associated with a gruesome story that explains the curiously named Hangman Stone Lane which runs through Leckhampstead from Chaddleworth to Boxford. Having stolen a sheep from a farmer at Chaddleworth, a local sheep rustler was travelling to Boxford with the awkward parcel slung over his shoulder with a rope which he held around his neck. Feeling the strain of carrying the great weight, the thief sat down on a large stone beside the road and fell into a deep sleep. However, the sheep struggled to get free and the man was hanged by the rope that had remained around his neck. His ghost is said to haunt the land and the boulder, known as the Hangman's stone, can still be seen beside the lane.

GREAT SHEFFORD   MAP 1 REF C9
4 miles SE of Lambourn on the A338

This quiet village in the Lambourn Valley, is home to **St Mary's Church** which, although the building itself is of no particular note, has the only original round tower in the county. Probably dating from Norman times, the church is reached along an avenue of lime trees and through a stone arch.

EASTBURY   MAP 1 REF B9
1½ miles SE of Lambourn off the B4000

This ancient village, again in the valley of the River Lambourn, was the home of John Estbury who, in 1502, founded the **Isbury Almshouses** at nearby Lambourn. The family had first acquired land in the area in the late 14th century and it is almost certain that they also gave the village its name. However, the name of the almshouses probably comes from the local pronunciation of the family name.

The village is also home to an interesting **dovecote**, constructed in 1620, which has nearly 1000 nesting boxes.

NEWBURY

This crossroads town has, for many years, dominated the rural area of West Berkshire. Prospering during the Middle Ages, and afterwards, on the importance of the woollen industry, the town became famous as **The Cloth Town**. Among the various characters who made their money out of the weaving of the wool the best known is Jack of Newbury (John Smallwood or Winchcombe), who died in 1519. Asked to raise two horsemen and two footmen for Henry VIII's campaign against the Scots, Jack raised 50 of each and led them himself. However, they only got as far as Stony Stratford in Buckinghamshire before news of the victory of Flodden reached them and they turned for home. In fact, Jack of Newbury was rather more than just a local merchant and his life story has become a local legend. Apprenticed to a rich Newbury clothmaker, when his master died, Jack married the widow and, upon her death, he inherited the wealthy business. Over the years he became one of the town's leading merchants employing as many as a thousand people. After displaying his loyalty to the king, Jack was offered a knighthood which he turned down on the grounds that he wanted to remain equal with his workers.

Evidence of the town's wealth can be seen in the splendid 'Wool' **Church of St Nicholas** which was constructed between 1500 and 1532. Built on the site of a Norman church, no expense was spared and Jack of Newbury gave the money for the magnificent five bayed nave. Unfortunately, the church has seen much restoration work, particularly during the Victorian age, but the fine pupil and elaborately decorated nave roof have survived.

During the Civil War there were two battles fought nearby, in 1643 and 1644, and following the war, the town's clothing industry declined. However, the 18th century saw the construction of turnpike roads and Newbury became a busy coaching stop on the road from London to Bath. The town further opened up to travellers and the needs of carriers with the completion of the **Kennet and Avon Canal** in 1810. **Newbury Lock**, built in 1796, was the first lock to be built along the canal and it is also the only one to have lever-operated ground paddles (the sluices that let in the water) which are known as *'Jack Cloughs'*.

Back in the centre of the town, in the Market Square is the **Newbury Museum**, housed in the 17th-century cloth hall and the adjacent 18th-century

Winning Post, Newbury Racecourse

granary, a store used by traders travelling the canal. As well as the archaeological section, the history of the town is fully explained, including the two battles of Newbury during the Civil War. Though much of the town centre dates from the Victorian age, there are some other interesting older buildings to be found. Aside from the Church of St Nicholas, visitors can see Lower Raymonds Buildings, a dignified row of almshouses dating from 1796, and the newer Upper Raymonds Buildings which were completed in 1826. Also in the area is St Bartholomew's Hospital, the town's oldest charitable institution, which was founded by King John though the building dates from the 17th century.

Just to the north of the town lies **Shaw House**, a splendid example of Elizabethan architecture and the finest in Berkshire, that dates from 1581. Built by a wealthy clothing merchant, Thomas Dolman, he chose to put his money into this elaborate house rather than his business, much to the displeasure of his workers. Though not open to the public, glimpses of the house can be seen from the road.

Those arriving in Newbury from the south will pass the Victorian **Falkland Memorial**, which should not be confused with the 1980s conflict in the South Atlantic. It is, in fact, a memorial to Lord Falkland who was killed at the first battle of Newbury in 1643. Finally, to the east of the town lies the first class **Newbury Racecourse** which offers both flat and National Hunt racing throughout the year.

Found down a quiet cul-de-sac close to the Kennet Canal, **Beaumont House** is a delightful guest house that is also well placed for the centre of Newbury and its station. Owned and personally run by Mrs Beaumont, a charming French lady who has lived here since the late 1970s, the accommodation in this comfortable house is excellent. There are five guest rooms, each with a dedicated bathroom, and, like the rest of the house,

Beaumont House, 4 St Johns Road, Newbury, Berks RG14 7LX Tel: 01635 47858

there is a distinct gallic atmosphere and style. Guests take their breakfast in the large conservatory, surrounded by orange trees and exotic plants, that also over-looks the beautifully maintained large town garden. Well decorated and furnished there is plenty of interesting and unusual bric a brac dotted around the house and guests should look out for the veteran rocking horse in the hall way.

Situated just outside Newbury, **The Five Bells** is a typical country pub with superb views from its rear garden over the Lambourn valley to Donnington Castle. A popular inn with locals, the pub is run by Carol and Dave John and, in the short time that they have been here, they have not only given the old

The Five Bells, Lambourn Road, Woodspeen, Newbury, Berks RG18 2NB
Tel: 01635 48763

building a facelift but also opened up the scenic garden, added a children's play area, and keep a Shetland pony to amuse the children. As well as being family orientated, this is certainly the place to come to for an excellent pint of real ale. As a member of CAMRA, the quality and choice of ales found behind the bar is assured and the addition of a delicious menu of bar meals and snacks ensures that no one goes home hungry. Comfortable accommodation too is available in a choice of either double or single rooms and, with the added attraction of a limo service, this is also an great place to stay whilst in the area or visiting the races.

AROUND NEWBURY

DONNINGTON
MAP 1 REF C10
1 mile N of Newbury on the B4494

Despite being so close to the town of Newbury, Donnington has managed to retain its village identity and atmosphere. To the west of the village, and visible from the road, is Donnington Grove House. Built in 1759 and designed by the architect John Chute, this was the home, in the late 18th century, of the Brummell family and Beau Brummell, the instigator of the Bath Society, lived here as a child.

However, most visitors to the village come to see the **Donnington Castle**, a late 14th-century defence that was built by Sir Richard Abberbury. Once a magnificent structure, only the twin towered gatehouse survives amidst the impressive earthworks. Owned by English Heritage, the castle had its most eventful period during the Civil War when it was the scene of one of the longest

Donnington Castle

sieges of the conflict. Charles I's troops were held here for 20 months and this was the time when most of the castle was destroyed. During the second of the two battles of Newbury, Charles I stayed at nearby Shaw House, whilst Sir John Boys defended the castle.

WINTERBOURNE

MAP 1 REF C9

3 miles N of Newbury off the B4494

Just south of the village lies **Snelsmore Common Country Park**, one of the county's most important natural history sites. The common comprises a range of different habitats, including woodland, heathland, and bog, and it supports a correspondingly wide variety of plant and animal life.

CURRIDGE

MAP 1 REF D9

3 miles N of Newbury off the B4009

This small village has an interesting **village school** that was founded on land leased from the Dean and Chapter of Westminster, by two sisters Miss Mary Wasey and Mrs Jane Stackpole. Built in 1856, the school was also designed to act as the village church and each Sunday the interior was transformed into a place of worship. Though the Education Board tried to take over and erected another, larger, school building in the village, Miss Wasey, paid to keep the school going until her death in 1880. The situation continued right up until 1965, when the building was deconsecrated and services were moved to the parish church in neighbouring Hermitage.

Found in the heart of the Lambourn Valley in this small village, **The Bunk Inn** is a tucked away pub and restaurant that is well worth seeking out. Surrounded by farmland, The Bunk is ideally situated, very popular, and locally

The Bunk Inn, Curridge Village, near Hermitage, Newbury, Berks RG18 9DS Tel: 01635 200400 Fax: 01635 200336

renowned. Owned and personally run by the Liquorish family which comprises Michael Liquorish, his partner Ali, father Jack, and mother Mrs Micky, this successful family inn is a charming place to find. As well as serving a wide range of real and cask ales and beers, there is a fine selection of wines, brandies, ports, and whiskies that compliment the delicious food that has helped The Bunk gain such an enviable reputation. There are two restaurant areas within the pub, which though they are small and intimate have, with clever use of conservatory style windows and ceilings, created a light and airy atmosphere. Indeed, during the summer great use is made of both the front and back patio areas for al fresco dining. Booking a table, especially at the weekends, is advisable due to its popularity. Those worried about getting lost finding The Bunk can phone for a map before setting off.

HERMITAGE
MAP 1 REF D9
4 miles NE of Newbury on the B4009

Found just to the east, in the village of Hermitage, and hidden within extensive woodland grounds is **Yaffles**, the home of Jean and Tony Bradford who offer magnificent self-catering accommodation in this most tranquil and relaxing of places. Very much off the beaten track and yet ideally placed for touring the area, guests have a choice of two outstanding units. Both the Garden Flat and the Studio, a converted stable block, are built, equipped, and furnished to the highest of standards and the accommodation they provide is certainly second to none. The larger of the two, the Garden Flat, is found some distance from

Yaffles, Red Shute Hill, Hermitage, Berks RG18 9QH
Tel/Fax: 01635 201100

the main house and as well as having two comfortable en-suite bedrooms, there is also a modern kitchen with dining room area and a spacious lounge with panoramic views over the garden from the large picture window. The accommodation provided by the one bedroom studio is of the same excellent standard and both units have good heating. Yaffles is the ideal place to stay for those looking for peace and quiet within a luxurious setting.

BUCKLEBURY   Map 1 ref D9
5 miles NE of Newbury off the B4009

This quiet hamlet lies on the banks of the River Pang and its most interesting feature is the **Church of St Mary**, with its splendid Norman doorway. Up until the time of the Dissolution the manor of Bucklebury had belonged to Reading Abbey, but, in 1540, it came into the hands of John Winchcombe, the son of Jack of Newbury. By the late 17th century the manor had passed to Frances Winchcombe, who married Henry St John, the 1st Lord Bolingbroke. Bolingbroke was the Secretary of State to Queen Anne. Following her death and having run through his wife's fortune, he fled to France, leaving his wife in Berkshire. Broken-hearted and in debt, Frances died at the age of 39 and her ghost is said to haunt the area in an open carriage pulled by black horses.

COLD ASH   Map 1 ref D10
3 miles NE of Newbury off the B4009

Just to the west lies the village of Cold Ash where Nick and Maggie Hex are the hosts at **The Castle Inn**, a 19th-century inn that offers both visitors and locals

The Castle Inn, Cold Ash Hill, Cold Ash, Newbury, Berks RG18 9PS
Tel: 01635 863232

a warm, friendly welcome. Cosy and comfortable (with an open log fire in the winter), the interior of the inn has recently been refurbished but it has lost none of its Victorian charm and, as well as the large bar area, there are numerous alcoves that provide customers with a more intimate place to eat and enjoy a drink. The low ceilings, dark beams, and a gleaming display of brassware all add to the atmosphere at The Castle Inn. From the long L-shaped bar a range of real ales - the guest beers change monthly - and a good selection of house wines are served whilst those requiring more solid refreshment will find excellent value-for-money blackboard menus every lunchtime and every evening (except Monday). With separate vegetarian, curry, and grill menus, a very popular Sunday lunch (booking is essential), an appetising range of bar snacks, and the famous mixed grill, this is an excellent pub that caters for everyone. During the summer, the south facing terrace really comes into its own as not only is it a superb sun trap but the flower-filled hanging baskets and window boxes make it a really colourful place to sit and enjoy the delicious food and drink.

THATCHAM
MAP 1 REF D10

2 miles E of Newbury on the A4

Believed to be the oldest village in Britain, it is hard to imagine that this now large suburb of Newbury was once a small place. **Thatcham Moor** is one of the largest areas of inland freshwater reed beds in the country and, as well as the reeds which can grow up to six feet in height, the area supports numerous species of marshland and aquatic plants. Birds too abound here and it is an important breeding ground for reed and sedge warblers.

GREENHAM
MAP 1 REF D10

1½ miles S of Newbury off the A34

This village, which is now more a suburb of Newbury, is famous for the American Airbase that occupied the large common around the perimeter of which the Greenham Common Women made a permanent camp and protested against nuclear weaponry.

BISHOPS GREEN
MAP 1 REF D10

3 miles S of Newbury off the A339

Just a couple of miles southeast of Newbury, and close to the county border with Hampshire, lies the village of Bishops Green. Situated within 50 acres of grassland and rolling countryside, yet close enough to Newbury, **Bishops Green Farm Campsite and Fishing** is the ideal place to get away from it all. Nick Smith, who has been here over 35 years, is helped by his long suffering partner Mary, and, though they are from farming families, this friendly couple now concentrate on the fishing and camping side of the business.

Bishops Green Farm Campsite and Fishing, Bishops Green Farm, Bishops Green, near Newbury, Berks RG20 4JP Tel: 01635 268365

This campsite with modern amenities is level, sheltered and well kept. Campers are welcome to walk most of the farm and woodland through which the River Enborne flows. The one and a half acre coarse fishing lake supports roach, tench, and many double figured carp. The lake is fished on a day ticket basis. Bishops Green Farm Campsite and Fishing is the perfect place for a quiet holiday with all of Berkshire's attractions within easy reach.

BURGHCLERE   MAP 1 REF C10
4 miles S of Newbury off A34

The village is home to the **Sandham Memorial Chapel**, which was built in the 1920s to remember the dead of World War I. What, however, makes this chapel so interesting are the internal murals which entirely cover the walls that are considered by many to be Stanley Spencer's greatest achievement. An extraordinary project, the murals illustrate the artist's experiences as a medical orderly during the war and he celebrates the everyday routine of a soldier's life. The pictures reach a climax with the huge *'Resurrection of the Soldiers'* which completely fills the east wall. This modern chapel is found amidst beautiful and tranquil scenery with views across **Watership Down**.

With a large and attractive garden overlooking Watership Down country, **The Carpenters Arms** is the ideal place to stop for some refreshment whilst visiting the area and families, particularly, are welcome. Built in 1820, the pub building has retained many of its original features and the open log fire in the lounge bar certainly adds to the warm and cosy feel of this typical country inn. With over 25 year experience in the trade, landlord and lady, Christopher and Audrey Ayling, with the help of their daughter Fiona, are very well placed to provide all customers, both locals and visitors, with a friendly welcome and some superb hospitality. With a good range of real ales and a fine selection of wines available, the high standard of the drinks served here is matched by the

**The Carpenters Arms, Harts Lane, Burghclere, Berks RG20 9JY
Tel: 01635 278251**

tasty and delicious menu of bar snacks and restaurant meals that are also served. The intimate conservatory restaurant area is not only a pleasant place for a quiet and relaxing dinner but it is also popular on Sundays when the traditional roast lunch, a house speciality, is served. The summer sees many of the pub's patrons moving from the cosy interior out into the flower-filled garden and patio areas where the regular barbecues prove to be another popular feature of this excellent establishment. Finally, one further attraction is the Stanley Spencer Memorial Chapel, with its collection of paintings, that lies just 100 yards or so from the pub.

COMBE   MAP 1 REF B10
7½ miles SW of Newbury off A338

This isolated hamlet, in the southwest corner of the county, is overlooked by **Walbury Hill** which, at 974 feet is the highest point in Berkshire. A popular place for walking and hang-gliding, the hill not only offers excellent panoramic views but there is also an Iron Age hill fort on its summit.

Close to the hill lies **Combe Gibbet**, one of the last public hanging places in the country. Originally erected for a couple who had committed murder, the gallows have a crossbar with a his and hers side.

INKPEN   MAP 1 REF B10
7 miles SW of Newbury off the A338

The village lies below the steep chalk ridge which separates the Thames basin from Hampshire. **Inkpen Common**, to the east of the village, is a Site of Special Scientific Interest where there is, amongst the heath and woodland, a wet valley bog and pond created from an old clay pit. As well as the unusual collection of plants, this is a popular breeding site for many birds and there is also an abundance of butterflies.

Found in the heart of the countryside, **The Swan Inn** is a charming 17th-century inn that is certainly more than it would first appear to be. The Swan Inn was purchased by Mary and Bernard Harris in 1996 and, during the past three years, they have turned the inn and adjacent buildings into a real haven for both visitors and locals. Open seven days a week, the menu covers everything from bar snacks to full à la carte in the organic restaurant. As well as

The Swan Inn, Lower Green, Inkpen, Hungerford, Berks RG17 9DX
Tel: 01488 668326

ensuring that all the dishes are prepared from the very best ingredients, there is also a wide range of vegetarian options. There are four excellent real ales and The Swan Inn features in the CAMRA Good Beer Guide.

Popular with locals, The Swan Inn is a well known stopping place for walkers and all those travelling in the area, whether on foot, cycling, or in a car will be glad to hear that comfortable accommodation is also available here. The inn has 10 charming en-suite guest rooms. Finally, adjoining the pub, but with a separate entrance, is a shop that will be of great use to walkers and those new to the area. As well as stocking organic produce, maps, and guide books, there is a range of craft items and paintings by local artists on sale.

HUNGERFORD   MAP 1 REF B10
8 miles W of Hungerford on the A4

Although not mentioned in the Domesday Book, by the Middle Ages this old market town was well established and the manor of Hungerford had some distinguished lords including Simon de Montford and John of Gaunt. A quiet and peaceful place, Hungerford's heyday came in the 18th century when the turnpike road from London to Bath, which passes through the town, was built. By 1840, the town had eight coaching inns serving the needs of travellers and the prosperity continued with the opening of the **Kennet and Avon Canal** but the building of the railway took much of the trade away and the town reverted back, once more, to its early, gentle lifestyle. However, several of the old coaching inns have survived and, in particular, The Bear Hotel. Although it has an impressive Georgian frontage , the building actually dates back to 1494, making it one of the oldest in the town. It was here, in 1688, that a meeting took place between William of Orange and representatives of James II which culminated in the end of the House of Stuart and the flight of James II to France.

As well as still holding a weekly market, the town also continues the ancient tradition known as the *Hocktide Festival* or *Tutti Day* (tutti meaning a bunch of flowers). Held every year on the second Tuesday after Easter, the festival was originally used as a means of collecting an early form of council tax. During the colourful event, two men carrying a six foot pole decorated with ribbons and flowers go around each household collecting the tax. To ease the burden of their visit, the men share a drink with the man of the house, give him an orange, and kiss his wife before collecting their penny payment. Today, however, though the visits are made no money is collected.

For a place off the beaten track, in more ways than one, **Little Hidden Farm** is certainly the place to seek out. Owned by two nature lovers, Susan and Bill Acworth, since the mid 1980s, this 150-acre mixed farm is still very much a working farm which takes up most of Bill's time. However, Bill also works as a consultant on environmental and conservation issues and anyone interested in making use of his knowledge and expertise is requested to contact Bill by telephone.

In a departure from more conventional farming the couple, on receiving a grant, have turned several of their pastures into wild flower meadows through which there are peaceful and interesting walks. Over 50 different species of wild flowers have been planted and the meadows form an important living library of British wild plants. Though these meadows are a welcome sight in themselves they are not just ornamental as both the plants and the seeds are sold from the farm.

Susan too has a great love of the countryside and conservation though her particular expertise is pastel painting and horse riding. By prior arrangement over the telephone, visitors with some riding ability can take advantage of Susan's

Little Hidden Farm, Wantage Road, Hungerford, Berks RG17 0PN
Tel: 01488 683253

riding school from where hacks are made around the farm and through the surrounding countryside.

WICKHAM   MAP 1 REF C9
5½ miles NW of Newbury off the B4000

Although the parish **Church of St Swithun**, in this rural village, was almost completely rebuilt in the 1840s by Bejamin Ferrey, the tower retains its original Anglo Saxon bottom half (the rest being Victorian) which makes it unique amongst Berkshire churches. Inside, too, there is an unusual feature: a series of papier-mâché elephants which appear to hold up the aisle roof. Bought at the Paris Exhibition of 1862, they were intended for the rectory but, as they were to large, ended up in the church.

BOXFORD   MAP 1 REF C9
4 miles NW of Newbury of the B4000

The charming Berkshire village, in the Lambourn Valley, presents an idyllic rural scene as it has several thatched cottages and a picturesque gabled watermill beside the brook. However, all has not been peaceful in this quiet village as, in the late 17th century a Quaker, Oliver Sansom feuded with the vicar. The quarrel continued for some time and, when the church tower collapsed into Sansom's garden, he kept the stones as he saw them as a gift from heaven. It was, though, the vicar who had the last word for he had Sansom jailed for not attending church.

2 In and Around Reading

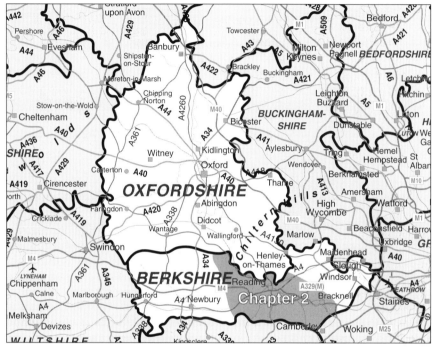

Reading dominates this central region of Berkshire: a thriving commuter town with excellent links both to London and the west. However, although the town may, at first glance, seem to be very much a product of the 19th and 20th centuries, there has been a settlement here for many years and the remains of its Abbey can still be seen in Forbury Gardens. Perhaps, though, the town is best known for the imprisonment, in its jail, of the Victorian playwright and poet Oscar Wilde.

Water too dominates this area of Berkshire as the two main waterways, the River Thames and the Kennet and Avon Canal, join together at Reading. The Thames, forming the northern county border with Oxfordshire, has, along its southern banks, many delightful riverside villages where, naturally, boating has been a key feature for many years. The Victorian and Edwardian passion for the river has lead to the growth of many of the villages as fashionable places for a day trip or short holiday and they remain pleasurable places to visit today.

To the south, the Kennet and Avon Canal provides another insight into the days before road and rail travel became the norm for freight. Very much a working canal, linking London with the west, the visitor centre at Aldermaston Wharf offers visitors the chance to relive the lives of those working the waterway.

READING

This thriving commuter town is a delightful combination of over a thousand years of history and a vibrant and modern city. There are Victorian brick buildings nestling beside beautiful medieval churches, famous coaching inns opposite high tech offices and some of the best shopping in the area. However, Reading began as a Saxon settlement between the Rivers Thames and Kennet. A defensible site, it was used by the Danes as a base for their attack on Wessex in the 9th century.

The town grew up around its **Abbey**, which was founded in 1121 by Henry I, the youngest son of William the Conqueror, and it was consecrated by Thomas à Becket in 1164. The abbey went on to become one of the most important religious houses - its relics include a piece of Jesus' shoe, the tooth of St Luke, and a slice of Moses' rod - and parliament were known to meet here on occasions. As Henry I is also buried here, Reading is one of only a handful of towns where Kings of England have been laid to rest. Today, the abbey ruins can be found in **Forbury Gardens** on the banks of the River Kennet. Fortunately, some of the abbey's wonderful architecture can still be seen and, in particular, there is St Laurence's Church and the abbey Gatehouse. The Gatehouse was, after the Reformation, turned into a school and, in 1785, Jane Austen was a pupil here. The gardens are also home to the **Maiwand Lion**, which commemorates the men of the Berkshire Regiment who died in the Afghan Campaign of 1879.

Another originally Norman building in the town is **St Mary's Church**, the south arcade of which dates from around 1200. The most attractive feature here is the church tower: erected in 1550 it is of a high distinguished chequerboard pattern which uses stone blocks and flint panels.

Adjacent to the abbey ruins is another of Reading's famous buildings - **Reading Prison**. Hardly a tourist attraction, it was here that Oscar Wilde was imprisoned and where he wrote *De Produnis*. His confinement here also inspired the writer to compose the epic *Ballad of Reading Gaol* whilst staying in Paris in 1898.

Though the town developed during the Middle Ages as a result of a flourishing woollen industry, it was during the 18th century with the coming of both the turnpike roads and the opening of the **Kennet and Avon Canal** which saw the town boom. By the 19th century, Reading was known for its three Bs: beer,

St Mary's Church, Reading

bulbs, and biscuits. As the trade of the canal and River Thames increased, the movement of corn and malt explains the growth of the brewing trade here whilst bulbs is a reference to Sutton Seeds who were founded here in 1806. The world renowned biscuit-making firm of Huntley and Palmer began life here in 1826, when Joseph Huntley founded the firm, to be joined, in 1841, by George Palmer, inventor of the stamping machine.

The Story of Reading, a permanent exhibition at the **Reading Museum**, is the ideal place to gain a full understanding of the history of the town, from the earliest times to the present day. Here, too, can be seen the world's only full size replica of the Bayeux Tapestry, made in the 19th century and which features Edward the Confessor, once Lord of the Royal Manor in Reading, as a central figure. As a contrast to the museum's displays depicting the life of the town in the 20th century, The Silchester Gallery is devoted to the describing day to day life at Calleva Atrebatum, the Roman town of Silchester, using Roman artefacts unearthed there during early excavations.

Situated on the banks of the River Kennet and housed in a range of canal buildings, **Blake's Lock Museum** describes the life of the town in the 19th and early 20th centuries. Originally part of a pumping station built at Blake's Weir in the 1870s, the buildings themselves are also of interest and are superb exam-

Blake's Lock Museum, Reading

ples of Victorian industrial architecture combined with decorative Reading brick-work. As well as covering the town's close links with its waterways and the part they played in Reading's prosperity, visitors can wander around the reconstructed shops and workshops.

Finally, founded in 1892 Reading Extension College took the examinations of the University of London until 1925 when the college became a university in its own right. Lying to the south of the town centre, the university campus is home to the **Museum of English Rural Life**, where not only is there a splendid wagon collection but also displays covering farm tools, machinery, and equipment, as well as rural crafts.

AROUND READING

CAVERSHAM   Map 2 ref F9
1 mile N of Reading on the A4155

Until 1911, this quiet village, across the River Thames from Reading, was in Oxfordshire but, once the county boundary changed there has been little to prevent Caversham becoming a suburb of the town. An old settlement, in the Middle Ages, Caversham was an important place of pilgrimage with visitors travelling from far and wide to visit St Anne's Well where, they believed, their ailments would be cured.

SONNING   MAP 2 REF F9
3 miles NE of Reading off the A4

This attractive little village, which leads down to the River Thames, is a popular
place for visitors especially during the summer weekends. An ancient place, the
Norman church, which was heavily restored in the 19th century, almost certainly stands on the site of a Saxon building and, just to the south, was once a
palace belonging to the Bishops of Salisbury. In 1399, after he had been de-
posed, Richard II brought his young bride, Isabella, here to be looked after by
the bishop and her ghost is said to walk the paths beside the river.

However, the queen is not the only famous resident of Sonning as, on Grove
Street, lies **Turpin's**, a house which once belonged to Dick Turpin's aunt and
where the notorious highwayman occasionally took refuge. Behind the wall of
the old bishop's palace, and well hidden from passers-by, is **Deanery Gardens**,
the house of Edward Hudson, the owner of *Country Life*, which was built in
1901 to the designs of Sir Edwin Lutyens.

Crossing the river by the superb 18th-century bridge not only brings the
visitor into the county of Oxfordshire but also to an old mill which has been
turned into a magnificent restaurant and theatre.

WOODLEY   MAP 2 REF F9
3 miles E of Reading off the A4

Found on the site of Woodley airfield, once a thriving centre of the aircraft
industry, the **Museum of Berkshire Aviation** reconstructs and exhibits Miles
and Handley Page aircraft. As well as the aeroplanes, which including a Handley
Page Herald, a Miles Magister, and a Fairey Gyrodyne, there is a wind tunnel
model for the first ever supersonic aircraft and numerous pictorial records and
priceless archives to see.

HURST   MAP 2 REF G9
4½ miles E of Reading off the A321

This attractive, scattered village is home to a Norman church, well endowed
with monuments, and facing which there are some 17th century almshouses.
The village bowling green is said to have been made for Charles II though there
is little evidence to support this claim.

Just to the south lies **Dinton Pastures Country Park**, a large area of lakes,
rivers, hedgerows, and meadows rich in wildlife. Until the 1970s, this area was
excavated for sand and gravel, but the former pits are now attractive lakes and
ponds: one of which has been stocked for coarse fishing and the largest is set
aside for canoeing and windsurfing.

Found in the heart of this country village, **The Green Man** is a charming
17th-century Brakspear inn that is owned and personally run by father and son,

The Green Man, Hinton Road, Hurst, Twyford, Berks RG10 0BP
Tel: 0118 934 2599

Gordon and Simon Guile. Very much an English country inn, the interior of the pub retains many of the building's original features including the low ceilings, exposed beams, and the wall timbers. Throughout the open plan bar there are several different areas but all are comfortably furnished and the numerous old photographs and prints on the walls add to the overall cosy ambience. An excellent place for a drink, The Green Man is also well known for the high quality of the meals that are served there each day. As the family name is French, customers will not be surprised to find that there is a strong French influence in the wide variety of dishes served and each is prepared and presented with style and flair. Fish too features heavily and, on celebratory days, such as St George's Day, the menu changes to reflect the anniversary. Along with the well chosen menu there is an interesting and well priced wine list that not only includes wines from around the world but also from the Thames Valley. Finally, to the rear of this attractive old inn there is a lovely patio area, ideal for the summer, which includes overhead heating to keep customers warm as the evenings grow chilly.

WOKINGHAM
MAP 2 REF G10

6 miles SE of Reading on the A329

This largely residential town has, at its centre, an old triangular market place where too can be found the amusing triangular **Town Hall** built in 1860. Amidst the mainly Victorian town centre, there are some attractive Georgian buildings whilst the parish Church of All Saints is older still, having been built in medieval times.

However, the town's most attractive building is **Lucas Hospital**, located to the south of the town centre. Originally almshouses, built in 1666, they were founded by Henry Lucas, a mathematician and Member of Parliament for Cambridge University. Today, the hospital still cares for elderly though now in the style of a retirement home but it can be visited by appointment with the resident matron.

BARKHAM
Map 2 ref G10

5½ miles SE of Reading off the A327

The oldest village in the area, Barkham was mentioned in the Domesday Book and it also once formed the boundary of Henry VIII's hunting forest. The parish **Church of St James** stands on an ancient site, where visiting monks crossed the downs, and it chalice dates from the time of Charles I. During the Commonwealth, the chalice, along with other church silver, was hidden in the village pond and was only restored to the church when Charles II came to the throne. Between 1782 and 1819, the Rev David Davies was the rector here and, whilst at Barkham, he wrote *The Case of Labourers in Husbandry*. This classic study of the poor conditions of farm labourers in the village in the 18th century was also a call for fair wages and rural social reform. Another rector of the village, Rev PH Ditchfield (here from 1886 to 1930) also took to writing though in this case Ditchfield concentrated on rural England and the history of Berkshire.

To the west of the village lie **The Coombes**, woodland which was once part of Windsor Forest and is now in private ownership. However, there are a number of public rights of way through the woods and they make a particularly delightful walk during the spring.

FINCHAMPSTEAD
Map 2 ref G10

8 miles S of Reading off the A327

To the east of the village lie **Finchampstead Ridges**, now owned by the National Trust and from which there are wonderful views across the Blackwater Valley. Ideal for informal walking, in 1863, John Walters constructed a road over the Ridges and, in 1869, it was planted with Wellingtonia (otherwise known as Giant Sequoia). The world's largest trees, they can grow to over 350 feet high and live for 4000 years and, although not native to Europe, they have grown here to a height of around 160 feet. As well as having a thicker softer bark than the native Scots Pine, they also hold their cones for around 20 years before they drop.

ARBORFIELD
Map 2 ref F10

4½ miles S of Reading on the A327

This is a village in three parts: Arborfield, home to the parish church; **Arborfield Cross**, on the crossroads; and **Arborfield Garrison**, where the Royal Electrical and Mechanical Engineers are based. Known as REME, the corps' task has been to maintain and recover all the army's equipment, from tanks to dentists drills and the **Royal Electrical and Mechanical Engineers' Museum** has displays on not only the valuable role the corps have played over the years but also the wide range of items they have recovered in that time.

Just to the south lies **California Country Park**, a wonderful, wooded beauty spot which also offers the visitor a wide variety of activities and landscapes. There is plenty of open space whilst the woods, with their 34 different species of tree, and the bogland provide a range of habitats for the many animals, plants, and birds that can be found here.

Found on the main road in the southern suburb of Reading, Arborfield Cross, **The Swan Inn** is an attractive black and white timber-framed 16th century coaching inn. A popular haunt of real ale drinkers, as well as locals and visitors passing through, all customers received a warm and friendly welcome from hosts Barbara and David Woodwards. As charming and full of character inside

The Swan Inn, Eversley Road, Arborfield Cross, near Reading, Berks RG2 9PQ Tel: 01189 760475

as the exterior would suggest, this old building has retained much of its old world appeal. There are low ceilings, exposed beams and the addition of pewter mugs, brasses, and a mass of old photographs and prints enhances the cosy, time standing still feel. As well as relaxing in the bar over a pint of well kept ale, customers can also enjoy a delicious meal from the traditional menu of excellent home-cooked fare that all comes under Barbara's supervision. Lovers of sport will not go short here either as, in the pub's function room, there is a big screen television for armchair fans to congregate around.

SHINFIELD
Map 2 ref F10

3 miles S of Reading on the A327

Dating back to Norman times, **St Mary's Church** has altered much over the years and the whole building, including the 17th century tower, was restored by Sir George Gilbert Scott in 1857. In the churchyard, close to the porch, is the gravestone of Louisa Parsons, who died in 1916 and was buried with full military honours. A nursing sister in the British Army, Louisa trained at the Nightingale School of Nursing at St Thomas' Hospital, London, and went on to have an astonishing career for a woman of her times, serving in several military campaigns all over the world. She also founded the University of Maryland Training School, which today remains a revered nursing college in the USA.

SWALLOWFIELD
Map 2 ref F10

5 miles S of Reading off the A33

This ancient settlement has been inhabited since prehistoric times and, by 1071, the manor was held by Roger de Breteuil, the originator of the Domesday Survey. Since then, the manor house, **Swallowfield Park**, has been associated with both royalty and notable personalities. The present house (unfortunately now all but a shell) was built in 1678 by Wren's assistant William Talman, for the 2nd Earl of Clarendon who acquired the estate upon marrying the heiress. In 1719, the park was purchased by Thomas Pitt, a former Governor of Madras, who used the proceeds of the sale of a large diamond he bought whilst out in India. The diamond can now be seen in the Louvre Museum, Paris, and Pitt's story was the basis of the novel, *The Moonstone*, by the author Wilkie Collins, who visited the house in 1860. The Italian Doorway, by Talman, is probably the house's most outstanding remaining feature and it marks the entrance to the walled garden. Here can be found a dog's graveyard where one of Charles Dickens' dogs, was bequeathed to his friend and owner of the house, Sir Charles Russell, by the novelist.

Set in beautiful gardens beside the River Loddon, **The Mill House Restaurant and Hotel** is a superb family run establishment where guests can relax in the glorious surroundings. A splendid Georgian house, built in 1823 as part of the 1st Duke of Wellington's Stratfield estate, Mill House has been restored to its original grandeur and in many ways still has the atmosphere of a grand country home. Personally managed by owners Mark and Kim Pybus, the restaurant here is magnificent and, whether it is lunch or dinner, visitors are sure to enjoy the excellent menus that are prepared and served by the hotel's resident chef. Well known locally and highly regarded, The Mill House Restaurant has gained an

The Mill House Restaurant and Hotel, Swallowfield, near Reading, Berks RG7 1PY Tel: 0118 988 3124 Fax: 0118 988 5550

enviable reputation for delicious and interesting dishes that would certainly not be out of place in any London establishment. Those lucky enough to be staying at the hotel can not only take full advantage of the dining facilities but the splendour of the hotel's well proportion rooms. Each of the ten en-suite guest rooms is fully equipped with the extras today's modern traveller expects but they also have a charm and character that is often lacking elsewhere. Surrounding the hotel is the delightful garden, a mixture of formal and informal, that is floodlit at night. The Mill House Hotel is also licensed for wedding ceremonies and, with much experience in holding receptions, this makes it an ideal location for such an important day.

MORTIMER   MAP 2 REF E10
6½ miles SW of Reading off the A33

Although, at first glance, this village looks and seems to date from the 19th century, it has a long history and it takes its name from Ralf Mortimer who held the manor here in 1086. However, in the churchyard of **St Mary's Church**, can be found a rare Saxon tombstone, marking the burial place of Aegalward, the son of the lord of the manor, that was erected by Toki, an important and wealthy courtier to King Canute in the early 11th century. The present day church was built in 1866 under the patronage of John Benyon, the then Lord of the Manor. This though is probably the fifth church on the site and some Norman fragments from the original building, such as the stained glass window behind the organ, can still be seen.

Also in the village is one of the few remaining examples of Brunel's original station design (Mortimer Station) and the War Memorial that commemorates the 56 men of Mortimer who died during World War I.

Close by lies **Windmill Common**, which was so named in the 18th century when the Rev James Morgan arranged for a windmill and cottage to be built here. Following the Enclosure Act of 1804, the land passed back into the hands of the lord of the manor who went on to plant the common with Scots pine. By 1832, the trees were causing the miller great problems and he wrote: "It lays under the necessity to remove because the fir plantation has overgrown and keep the wind off the mill." Though the mill has now gone, the pine trees are still standing on the common.

Found on the main road through the village, **The Turners Arms** is a traditional village pub that started life as three cottages and became a pub in the 1860s. Though situated on the road, to the rear of the building is a delightful, secluded, and enclosed beer garden which can only add to the charm of the inn. Run by Belinda Routledge, with the help of her two grown up daughters, this is a popular place with both locals and visitors alike. Appealing to all ages, the interior of the pub contains plenty of comfortable seating so that patrons can enjoy their drinks in a leisurely manner and the walls are decorated with gleam-

The Turners Arms, Mortimer, Reading, Berks RG7 3TW
Tel: 0118 933 2961 Fax: 0118 933 1521

ing brasses, dried wild flowers, and numerous prints and photographs. As well as serving drinks, it is well worth taking the time to enjoy a meal from the pub's ever-changing menu. Seafood is certainly a speciality of the inn and, along with the daily specials, there is sure to be something to tempted everyone here.

ALDERMASTON
MAP 1 REF E10

9 miles SW of Reading on the A340

It was in this tranquil village, in 1840, that the William pear was first propagated by John Staid, the then village schoolmaster. First known as the Aldermaston pear, a cutting of the plant is believed to have been taken to Australia where is it now called the Bartlett pear. Still retaining much of its original 12th-century structure and with a splendid Norman door, the lovely **St Mary's Church** provides the setting for the York Mystery Cycle, nativity plays dating from the 14th century which are performed here each year. Using beautiful period costumes and contemporary music, including a piece written by William Byrd, the cycle lasts a week and the plays attract visitors from far and wide.

Another old custom still continued in the village is the auctioning of the grazing rights of Church Acres every three years. Using the ancient method of a candle auction, a pin, in this case a horseshoe nail, is inserted into the tallow of a candle one inch from the wick. The candle is lit while bidding takes place and the grazing rights go to the highest bidder as the pin drops out of the candle. Outside under a yew tree in the churchyard lies the grave of Maria Hale, formerly known as the Aldermaston witch. She was said to turn herself into a large brown hare and although the hare was never caught or killed, at one time a local keeper wounded it in the leg and from then on it was noticed that Maria Hale was lame!

Aldermaston Wharf

Close to the village there is a delightful walk along the Kennet and Avon Canal to **Aldermaston Wharf**. A Grade II listed structure of beautifully restored 18th-century scalloped brickwork, the wharf is home to the **Kennet and Avon Canal Visitor Centre**, where the canalman's cottage houses an exhibition on the canal with information on its leisure facilities.

More recent history has seen the famous protest marches of the1950s outside the Atomic Research Establishment, which though situated in the grounds of Aldermaston Court, rather mysteriously, does not feature on Ordnance Survey Maps.

WOOLHAMPTON
10 miles SW of Reading on the A4

MAP 1 REF E10

This tranquil village on the banks of the **Kennet and Avon Canal**, has had a watermill since the time of the Domesday Survey in 1086 and it was again mentioned in 1351, when the manor and mill was owned by the Knights Hospitallers. The present mill, which today has been converted into offices, was built in 1820 and further extended in 1875. Powered by a brook which runs into the Kennet, the mill was last used in 1930.

Built in 1714 and with the addition of a striking Dutch roof in the 1930s, **The Falmouth Arms** is a distinctive building in this quiet village that is hard to miss. Managed since 1996 by Mary and Christopher Scott, this attractive and popular inn is also a lively meeting place for residents of the village and those who live locally. Light and airy inside, the open plan bar, with a large fireplace

The Falmouth Arms, Bath Road, Woolhampton, Berks RG7 5RT
Tel: 0118 971 3202

at either end, is an excellent place to come to for a relaxing drink and to while away a couple of hours catching up on the local news. The numerous pictures and photographs on display, of the pub and the village through this century, are also a major talking point. Food too is very much on the menu here and customers can enjoy a wide range of tasty bar snacks and meals that are served throughout the day. As well as the monthly theme evenings, Christopher and Mary also provide their customers with lively entertainment in the form of music at the weekends and quiz nights. Finally, The Falmouth Arms, in the true tradition of an inn, has nine en-suite guest rooms that not only provide the overnight visitor with comfortable accommodation but they are also fitted with all the latest amenities.

THEALE
MAP 2 REF E9
5 miles W of Reading on the A4

This delightful old coaching village is dominated by the magnificent 19th-century **Holy Trinity Church**. A splendid monument to the architect, the building is very reminiscent of Salisbury Cathedral from the outside, particularly the west front where two pinnacled towers stand either side of the arched tower leading into the church. Inside too there is much to see from the colourful painted patterns on the walls and the vaulted nave roof, to the finely carved benches and New Testament scenes in the chancel windows.

The village of **Sunnyside**, close to Theale, also lies on the busy main road from Bath to London which runs through Reading. Old documents show that the present **Fox and Hounds Inn** was built in 1850, just a few of years after the

**Fox and Hounds, Station Road, Sunnyside, Theale, Reading,
Berks RG7 4BE Tel & Fax: 0118 930 2295**

land on which it now stands was leased to innkeeper, Jesse Stroud, by the then Earl of Shrewsbury and Waterford. This was, of course, well before the present landlord and landlady, Don and Sue Guppy, came here in 1996 but the traditions of offering warm and welcoming hospitality are very much alive here still. The old world charm of this delightful inn has also been retained following a recent modernisation and it remains full of character with old oak beams and blazing log fires in winter. However, the open plan style of the interior helps to create a sense of space that is enhanced by the in-keeping restaurant area extension.

The place to come to for excellent food and drink, not only do Sue and Don serve a fine selections of beers, ales, lagers, and wines from the bar but the extensive menu at the Fox and Hounds has something for everyone. A very popular place for lunch, this is also a super place for an evening out.

ENGLEFIELD
6 miles W of Reading off the A340

Map 2 ref E9

The privately owned **Englefield House** was originally built in the first Elizabethan era but was enlarged in 1860. Situated in seven acres of woodland and deer park, stone balustrades and staircases lead down through formal terraces, herbaceous borders, and rose gardens in what is a glorious setting. The delightful gardens are open all year round whilst the house is open only by appointment.

BRADFIELD
7 miles W of Reading off the A340

Map 1 ref E9

This wooded village, on the banks of the River Pang, is dominated by its church and public school both of which are the work of the mid-19th century squire and vicar. The Rev Thomas Stevens, believing the medieval **Church of St Andrew** to be beneath his station in life, employed Sir George Gilbert Scott to rebuilt it in 1848. After this success, Stevens then went on and founded **Bradfield College**, in 1850, to provide, in part, choristers for the church. On top of the college's chapel can be seen an unusual weather vane, of a schoolmaster in a cap and gown, which was made in 1951 in memory of Dr Gray, headmaster from 1880 to 1910.

YATTENDON
10 miles W of Reading off the M4

Map 1 ref D9

For many years Robert Bridges, the poet laureate, lived in the village at the manor house with his wife, the daughter of architect Alfred Waterhouse. Whilst here, Robert, along with Prof H Ellis Wooldridge, edited the *Yattendon Hymnal*, in the hope that old tunes that were in danger of being forgotten would survive.

ALDWORTH
Map 1 ref D9

11 miles NW of Reading on the B4009

The parish Church of St Mary is famous for housing the **Aldworth Giants** - the larger than life effigies of the de la Beche family which date back to the 14th century. The head of the family, Sir Philip, who lies here with eight other members of his family, was the Sheriff of Berkshire and valet to Edward II. Though now somewhat defaced the effigies were so legendary that the church was visited by Elizabeth I. Outside, in the churchyard, are the remains of a once magnificent 1000 year old yew tree that was sadly damaged in a storm.

Nearby, at **Little Aldworth**, the grave of the poet Laurence Binyon, who wrote the famous lines "At the going down of the sun and in the morning, we shall remember them," can

Church of St Mary, Aldworth

be seen in the churchyard and, opposite the Bell Inn, there is one of the deepest wells in the country. Topped by great beams, heavy cogs, and wheels, it is some 327 feet deep.

STREATLEY
Map 1 ref E8

9 miles NW of Reading of the A417

Situated on the opposite bank of the River Thames from Goring (and Oxfordshire), there is a pretty bridge which links the two and overlooks the busy Goring Lock. This section of the Thames is known as **Goring Gap**, a great cutting created in the chalk by the water, which separates the Chilterns and the Berkshire Downs. A climb up **Streatley Hill**, to the west of the village, gives the best views over the village, river, and the gap.

BASILDON
Map 1 ref E9
8 miles NW of Reading on the A417

This small village is the last resting place of the inventor and agricultural engineer, Jethro Tull, and his grave can be seen in the churchyard. Here too is a monument which commemorates the tragic drowning of two brothers. Outside the churchyard is a further memorial, a classic pavilion built in memory of his parents by the late Mr Childe-Beale which is, today, the focal point of **Beale Park**. Covering some 300 acres of ancient water meadow, the park is home to a wide range of birds and animals. There are carefully tendered small herds of unusual farm animals, including rare breeds of sheep and goats, Highland cattle, deer, and South American llama, over 120 species of birds living in their natural habitat, and a pets' corner for smaller children. However, the park's work is not confined to the keeping of animals and, as well as planting a **Community Woodland**, an ancient reed bed has been restored. The park's other main attraction housed in the pavilion is the **Model Boat Collection**, which is one of the finest of its kind.

However, the village's main feature is the National Trust owned **Basildon Park**, an elegant, classical house designed in the 18th century by Carr of York, which is undoubtedly Berkshire's foremost mansion. Built between 1776 and 1783 for Francis Sykes, an official of the East India Company, the house is almost text book in style though it does have the unusual addition of an Anglo-Indian room. The interior, finished by JB Papworth and restored to its original splendour after World War II, is rich in fine plaster work, pictures, and furniture and the rooms open to the public include the Octagon Room and a decorative Shell Room. If the name Basildon seems familiar it is probably as a result of the notepaper: the head of the papermaking firm of Dickinson visited the house and decided to use the name for the high quality paper.

PANGBOURNE
Map 2 ref E9
5½ miles NW of Reading on the A417

Situated at the confluence of the River Pang and the River Thames, the town grew up in the late 19th and early 20th centuries as a fashionable place to live. As a result there are several attractive Victorian and Edwardian villas to be seen including a row of ornate Victorian houses known as the Seven Deadly Sins. It was here that the author Kenneth Graham retired, living at **Church Cottage** beside the church. Graham married late in life and it was whilst living here that he wrote *The Wind in the Willows*, the original bedtime stories that he invented for his son which were based along the banks of the river between Pangbourne and Marlow.

Visitors to the town who cross the elegant iron bridge to neighbouring Whitchurch must still pay a toll, though now very small. The right to exact the toll has existed since 1792 and it is one of the very few surviving privately owned toll bridges. It was at **Whitchurch Lock** that the characters in Jerome K Jerome's *Three Men in a Boat* abandoned their craft, after a series of mishaps, and returned to London.

TIDMARSH
MAP 2 REF E9

5 miles W of Reading on the A340

On the banks of the River Pang, the village is home to one of the most remarkable churches in the county. As well as boasting the finest Norman doorway in Berkshire, **St Laurence's Church** has a bell turret supported on massive bracing timbers which stand inside the church. The decorations on the timbers were carved in the early 12th century by the vicar's wife to mirror the work on the superb doorway.

Found in the heart of the village, **The Greyhound** pub is a charming old inn that dates back to the 12th century. A distinctive timber framed building, still with a thatched roof, though the inn has been added to over the years, particularly to meet the needs of stagecoach travellers, it has lost none of its character. The recent refurbishment, which followed a fire in the upper storey, has left the inn much as it would have appeared to customers in days gone by. With low ceilings and exposed roof and wall timbers there is certainly a cosy atmosphere with a real olde worlde feel. Owned and personally run by Susan and Martin Ford, this is an excellent place to come to for a pleasant drink in one of the two delightful bar areas. However, The Greyhound is also highly regarded for the superb menu of delicious homecooked food that is served at both lunchtime

The Greyhound, The Street, Tidmarsh, Berks RG8 8ER
Tel: 0118 984 3557 Fax: 0118 984 1600

and in the evening. A tasty mix of traditional pub favourites and more exotic dishes, The Greyhound is a place well worth visiting by those who appreciate good hospitality.

SULHAM
Map 2 ref E9

4½ miles W of Reading off the A340

Reached by a wooded footpath from the village church, there is, on a hill overlooking the Sulham valley, an ancient pigeon tower. However, there is much local speculation regarding the origins of the tower with some believing it to have been built as a look out tower during the Napoleonic Wars. Perhaps, though, the best explanation of its construction is as a folly built by the Wilder family, the village's main landowners for over 300 years.

3 East Berkshire

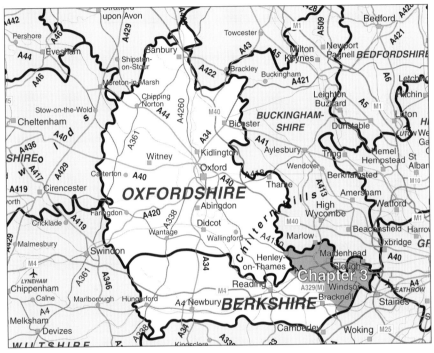

This western region of the Royal County of Berkshire is dominated by the 900 year presence of the Crown at Windsor. Building of the great castle was begun by William the Conqueror and, today, after the many additions and alterations over the centuries, it is a magnificent sight that provides a unique landmark for miles around. A major tourist attraction, whilst still being a royal residence, the castle is just one of the many places of interest which the small town of Windsor has to offer.

Across Windsor Great Park, the remains of the royal hunting forest, lies Ascot Racecourse. For one meeting each summer this is the place for the fashionable as people flock from all over the world to attend Royal Ascot but, for the rest of the year, this is an attractive and highly competitive course that was founded by Queen Anne in 1711.

The Thames also plays a great part in this area of Berkshire. There are numerous picturesque riverside towns and villages, several of which developed into fashionable riverside resorts during the Victorian era. Cookham, with its continuation of the ancient Swan Upping ceremony; Maidenhead, with the massive Boulter's Lock and Brunel's famous railway bridge; and Wraysbury, where King John signed the Magna Carta to appease the rebellious barons, are all places that not only exude history but provide pleasant walks along the river's banks.

WINDSOR

This old town grew up beneath the walls of the castle in a compact group of streets leading from the main entrance. Charming and full of character, this is a place of delightful timber-framed and Georgian houses and shop fronts, with riverside walks beside the Thames, and a wonderful racecourse. The elegant **Guildhall**, partly built by Wren in the 17th century, has an open ground floor for market stalls whilst the council chambers are on the first floor. Concerned that they might fall through the floor onto the stalls below the council members requested that Wren put in supporting pillars in the middle of the market hall. As his reassurances that the building was sound fell on deaf ears, Wren complied with their wishes but the pillars he built did not quite meet the ceiling - there by proving his point!

The grand central station, in the heart of the town, was built in 1897 to commemorate Queen Victoria's Diamond Jubilee and it is now home to a fascinating exhibition, **Royalty and Empire**, which charts the life and times of the country's longest reigning monarch. Close by, in the High Street, is another exhibition well worth visiting, **The Town and Crown Exhibition**. Here the development of the town and the influences of the Crown are explained in an imaginative and visual manner.

Meanwhile a trip to **The Dungeons of Windsor** provides a step back in time and an investigation of the town's history with a special regard for stories of crime and punishment from the early days of 13th-century lawlessness through to the harsh Victorian era. The Household Cavalry also have their home in Windsor, at Combermere Barracks, and here there is the superb **Household Cavalry Museum**, which displays collections of their uniforms, weapons, and armour from 1600 through to the present day.

In a perfect setting beside the River Thames, **Royal Windsor Racecourse** is one of the most attractive in the country. Though less grand than neighbouring Ascot, the summer evening meetings here are particularly enjoyable.

However, it is **Windsor Castle**, situated on Castle Hill, which draws thousands of tourists annually to this small town. The largest castle in the country and a royal residence for over 900 years, the castle was begun in the late 11th century by William the Conqueror as one in a chain of such defences which

Windsor Castle

stood on the approaches to London. Over the years various monarchs have added to the original typical Norman castle , the most notable additions being made by Henry VIII, Charles II, and George IV.

Various aspects of the castle are open to the public, in particular the sixteen state apartments which hold a remarkable collection of furniture, porcelain, and armour. Carvings by Grinling Gibbons are to be seen everywhere and the walls are adorned with a plethora of masterpieces, including paintings by Van Dyck and Rembrandt. On a somewhat smaller scale, but nonetheless impressive, is **Queen Mary's Dolls' House**. Designed by Sir Edwin Lutyens for Queen Mary, this is a perfect miniature palace, complete with working lifts and lights and also running water. Taking over three years to build, 1500 tradesmen were employed to ensure that every last detail was correct and the house was presented to the queen in 1924. In November 1992, a massive fire swept through the northeast corner of the castle and no-one in the country at the time will forget the incredible pictures of the great tower alight. After much restoration, the affected rooms, including the massive St George's Hall, the scene of many state banquets, have all been completed and are once again open to the public.

Windsor Castle is not just a defensive structure but it was also an ecclesiastical centre and, within its walls, is the magnificent **St George's Chapel**. Started by Edward IV in 1478, and taking some 50 years to finish, the chapel is not only one of the country's greatest religious buildings but also a wonderful example of the Perpendicular Gothic style. As well as being the last resting place of several monarchs, it is also the Chapel of the Most Noble Order of the Garter, Britain's highest order of chivalry.

Frogmore House, Windsor

Frogmore House, a modest manor house from the early 18th century, stands in Home Park, and over the years it has acted as a second, more relaxed royal residence than nearby Windsor Castle. During Queen Victoria's reign it was the home of her mother, the Duchess of Kent and now, famously, it is also home to the magnificent **Royal Mausoleum** dedicated to Prince Albert and also where Queen Victoria herself is buried beside her beloved husband. Only open to the public on two days in May, the mausoleum, in the delightful gardens laid out in the 1790s, remains a sombre yet restful place.

To the south of the town lies **Windsor Great Park**, a remnant of the once extensive Royal Hunting Forest, and a unique area of open parkland, woodland, and impressive views. The **Long Walk** stretches from the castle to **Snow Hill**, some three miles away, on top of which stands a huge bronze of George III on horseback put there in 1831. Queen Anne added the three mile ride to nearby Ascot race course. On the park's southern side lies **Smith's Lawn**, where polo matches are played most summer weekends. Windsor Great Park is also the setting for the Cartier International competition, polo's highlight event held every July, and the National Driving Championships.

First laid in 1931, **The Savill Garden**, created by Sir Eric Savill, is one of the best and finest woodland gardens to be seen anywhere. A garden for all seasons, there are colourful flower gardens, secret glades, and alpine meadows.

Finally, to the southwest and in 150 acres of parkland, is **Legoland Windsor**, where there are a whole range of amazing lego models on display which have been made from over 20 million bricks.

AROUND WINDSOR

ETON
MAP 2 REF H9

1 mile N of Windsor on the A355

Found just across the River Thames from Windsor, this town has grown up around **Eton College**, the famous public school that was founded in 1440 by Henry VI. Originally intended for 70 poor and worthy scholars and to educate students for the newly created King's College, at Cambridge University, the college has been added to greatly over the years. Of the original school buildings, only the College Hall and the kitchen have survived; the great gatehouse and Lupton's Tower were added in the 16th century and the Upper School dates from around 1690. However, the school has kept many ancient traditions over

Eton College, Eton

the years including the black tail mourning coats that were originally worn on the death of George III in 1820 and which are still worn today.

For centuries the college has educated the great and the good, including 19 prime ministers, artists, poets, and authors including William Pitt the Elder, Harold Macmillan, Thomas Gray (author of *Elegy Written in a Country Churchyard*), Henry Fielding, Shelly, George Orwell, and Ian Fleming. Eton has also been famous in the past for its strict discipline, personified in 1832 by a master who told the pupils when they rebelled: *"Boys, you must be pure of heart, for if not, I will thrash you until you are."*

SLOUGH
MAP 2 REF I8
2½ miles N of Windsor on the A355

At the turn of the last century, this was an insignificant settlement with a small population but, in 1920, a trading estate was created here and Slough grew rapidly - from 7000 people to around 100,000 today. For lovers of modern industrial architecture, this is an obvious place to make for but there is little to occupy those who do not. However, a trip to **Slough Museum**, which tells the story of the area from prehistoric times to the present day makes for an interesting and informative diversion.

DATCHET
MAP 2 REF I9
2 miles E of Windsor off the A308

The manor of Datchet dates back to the time of William the Conqueror who gave it, along with Ditton, to William, son of Ansculf. Having passed through several hands over the years, the manor is now with Lord Montagu of Beaulieu who, though he does not have a manor house here, does take part in the traditional 'Beating of the Bounds' which were first carried out in the 1634. An old custom designed to maintain and keep in good repair the manors boundaries, the event occurs every few years so that the position of the boundary can be passed from generation to generation.

WRAYSBURY
MAP 2 REF I9
3 miles SE of Windsor off the A308

Although **Magna Carta Island**, in the River Thames and where King John famously signed the document in 1215 for the rebellious baron, is a private island, there is a memorial to the site nearby. A stone tablet, found in the river during the 19th century, is reputed to be the table used for the signing.

Back in this riverside village, the ancient **Church of St Andrew** is certainly of interest. Dating mainly from the 13th century and built on the site of a Saxon church, the font has been used to baptise local infants for over 700 years. Among the various plaques on the floor of the chancel is a stone tablet to Edward Gould, a servant to Charles II who died 20 years after his master finally succeeded to the throne.

OLD WINDSOR
MAP 2 REF I9
2 miles SE of Windsor on the A308

A thriving Saxon settlement long before the Norman Conquest, when William the Conqueror decided to built his magnificent castle to the west, the town began to decline and has never regained its former importance. An attractive village today, the church and graveyard are full of memorials to a wide variety of famous and notable people. Worth looking out for is the effigy of Sir Charles

Murray, who presented the first hippopotamus to London Zoo; the box tomb of Mrs Brinsley Sheriden, wife of the 18th-century playwright; and the grave of the 18th-century actress Mary Robinson. Brought to the attention of the Prince of Wales, later George IV, for her roles in Shakespearean plays, Mary became his mistress in 1779 but, inevitably, he tired of her. Supporting herself by writing, she died in 1800, at the age of 42, and in poverty.

ASCOT   MAP 2 REF H10
6 miles SW of Windsor on the A329

A small village until 1711 when Queen Anne moved the Windsor race meeting to here and founded the world famous **Ascot Racecourse**. Its future secured when the Duke of Cumberland established a stud at Windsor in the 1750s, by the end of the century the meetings were being attended by Royalty on a regular basis. Today, Royal Ascot, held every June, is an international occasion of fashion and style with pageantry and tradition that is followed by racing enthusiasts world wide.

To the west of the now small town lies **Englemere Pond**, a Site of Special Scientific Interest and also a local nature reserve. Once part of the royal hunting ground which surrounded Windsor Castle and still owned by the Crown Estate, the main feature is the shallow acidic lake which offers a wide range of habitats from open water to marsh, for the many species of plants, birds, and animals, and insects found here

SANDHURST   MAP 2 REF G10
11 miles SW of Windsor on the A3095

The town is famous as being the home of the **Royal Military Academy**, the training place for army officers since it was established in 1907. The academy's **Staff College Museum** tells the history of officer training from its inception to the present day. Long before the academy was founded, in Saxon times, this settlement, in the valley of the River Blackwater, was part of the Parish of Sonning. Although there are no written records of a church having been here, in 1220, William de Wanda, Dean of Salisbury, visited a new and beautiful chapel at Sandhurst. The present Church of St Michael and All Angels, situated high above the River Blackwater, was built in 1853 to the designs of GE Street. However, it takes several old features from the previous church, including the Norman style doorway and an old beam supporting the wooden roof that is inscribed to Charles I and dated 1647.

Close by is **Trilakes**, a picturesque country park set in 18 acres and, naturally, there are lakes here. This is a wonderful place to visit with children as there are a wide assortment of pets and farm animals which they can get to know, including miniature horses, pygmy goats, donkeys, aviary birds, pot-bellied pigs and Soay sheep.

CROWTHORNE
MAP 2 REF G10

10 miles SW of Windsor on the B3348

A wild and virtually uninhabited part of the Royal Forest, Crowthorne only developed in the latter half of the 19th century when Wellington College and Broadmoor Hospital were established close by. At first a wooden church was erected but the present day, permanent building, was begun in 1872 following the designs of A Blomfield, the architect son of the Bishop of London. The Church of St John is a typical Victorian church of red brick dressed with Bath stone and, inside, there are courses of red and black brick.

Just to the east of the village lie the large buildings of **Broadmoor Hospital** which was founded in 1863. One of four special hospitals in the country it provides treatment for psychiatric patients under secure conditions.

BRACKNELL
MAP 2 REF G10

7 miles SW of Windsor on the A329

Designated a new town in 1948, Bracknell has developed quickly from a small place in poor sandy heathland into a large modern town with one of the first purpose built shopping centres in the country - opened in the 1960s. As well as being home to a number of high tech companies, Bracknell is also the home of the Meteorological Office.

However, the first mention of Bracknell has been traced back to a 10th-century Saxon document where, spelt as *Braccan Heal*, the name is thought to mean a piece of land belonging to Bracca. The community developed here at the junction of two major routes through Windsor Forest.

Seen from many parts of the town and a very prominent landmark is the centrally located **Bill Hill**. At the top of the hill can be found a circular mound of earth, hollowed out at the centre, which is all that remains of a Bronze Age round barrow. Used through out that period, these burial mounds, which may cover either individuals or groups, are the most common prehistoric monuments in the country even if this location, in the heart of a modern town, seems a little curious.

What remains of the great royal hunting ground, **Windsor Forest** (also called **Bracknell Forest**) lies to the south of the town and this vast area has over 30 parks and nature reserves and some 45 miles of footpaths and bridleways. Of particular interest in the area is **The Lookout Discovery Park**, an interactive science centre that brings to life the mysteries of both science and nature. Throughout the woodland surrounding the centre there are nature trails and walks to points of interest as well as the inappropriately named **Caesar's Camp**. Not a Roman fort, this camp is an Iron Age hill fort built over 2000 years ago but, close by, lies the Roman link road between London and Silchester. Locally known as the **Devil's Highway**, it is said to have acquired the name as the local inhabitants, after the Romans had left, thought that only the Devil could un-

Eastern Gateway to Caeser's Camp, Bracknell

dertake such a feat of engineering.

Also to the south of the town is the impressive **Coral Reef**, an indoor leisure pool with a tropical climate that provides family fun all year round.

WARFIELD   Map 2 ref H9
5½ miles W of Windsor off the A330

Originally a clearing in the forest, the village was given its name by Saxon settlers who also erected a wooden chapel here. However, by 1087, work had begun on a permanent building and St Michael's Church dates from that time. It has since doubled in size by additions made in the 14th and 15th centuries. Although the west tower is also thought to have been added at that time, it does not explain how a Norman window comes to be part of the tower's construction.

Nearby is the deserted medieval village of **Cruchfield** which, records show, had a manor here as early as 1186.

BINFIELD   Map 2 ref G9
8 miles SW of Windsor on the B3034

The village is famous as having been the boyhood home of the poet, Alexander Pope. After his father, a linen draper, had amassed a fortune, the family moved here and, as well as singing in the local choir, Pope gained a local following for his poems about the Windsor Forest and the River Loddon. To the south of the village lies **Pope's Wood**, a copse where the poet is said to have sought inspiration and, surrounding the wood, is **Pope's Meadow**, where not only are there pleasant walks but a wealth of animal and bird life supported by the wide variety of plants. Unfortunately little remains of the house in which he lived, though one room, his study, is said to have been preserved in the rebuilt Georgian manor house.

Other people associated with the village include the artist John Constable, who sketched the parish church whilst here towards the end of his honeymoon, and Miss Norah Wilmot ,who took over the training of horses in her father's local racing stable with great success.

Found in the centre of Binfield's shopping precinct, **V & A Traynor Fine Arts** is a pleasure to wander around. This delightful place, owned and personally run by Vincent and Ann Traynor since 1983, is a real treasure trove of paintings and prints, many of which have been created by local artists. An easy place to wander around and see the many different styles of artwork on offer, V & A Traynor Fine Arts is the ideal place to come to for that special present. As

V & A Traynor Fine Arts, 5 Oakmede Place, Terrace Road, Binfield, Berks RG42 4JF Tel: 01344 425508

well as selling a wide range of artwork, the shop stocks original pieces of pottery and the couple, who started out as picture framers, also sell hand-made frames. Anyone with an old and dirty picture may too be interested to know that picture restoration is another service offered by the couple.

WALTHAM ST LAWRENCE
7½ miles W of Windsor off the A4

MAP 2 REF G9

One of the most attractive villages in Berkshire, there is a charming Norman church and, close by, a wonderful 14th-century timber-framed inn. The village green too is still very much as it has been for centuries although the village pound has been replaced by a fence and some ash trees.

TWYFORD
10 miles W of Windsor on the A4

MAP 2 REF G9

Situated on the banks of the River Loddon and also with two streams, from which the town takes its name, it is not surprising that the town has had several watermills down the centuries. The first recorded mill is dated 1363 although there was mention of a miller as early as 1163. In 1799, a miller from Macclesfield, Thomas Billinge, came to the town and, among the several properties that he bought, was a grist mill. Here, Billinge and his wife set up a silk mill and, whilst other local silk mills were closing due to the competition from abroad, the silk mill at Twyford rode the storm and continued until 1845.

Returning to the task of milling flour, the water mill was then beset by several disastrous fires and, it was finally destroyed, by fire, in 1976. The replacement modern mill is certainly not as attractive as the previous buildings but it does continue the milling tradition in the town.

Found on the main road, in the village of **Hare Hatch**, just northeast of Twyford, **Ladds Garden Village** supplies everything for the garden imaginable. This is a popular place with people from a wide surrounding area and offers all manner of plants from seeds through to established trees and from vegetables through to roses and bedding plants. With a colourful display from early spring to late autumn the centre will be an inspiration to anyone looking to

**Ladds Garden Village, Bath Road, Hare Hatch, Reading,
Berks RG10 9SB Tel: 0118 940 4794**

liven up their garden. On site there is an aquatic centre providing a full range of fish, reptiles and accessories together with a florist offering a wide selection of houseplants and cut flowers.

Apart from all things that grow, the centre stocks a full range of gardening equipment, including garden sheds, and the display of excellent garden furniture not only suits every occasion but every pocket too. In addition to hardy outdoor tables and chairs there is also a fine selection of indoor wicker furniture that is ideal for the conservatory or summer house. Family pets and wild birds are not forgotten here with a pet shop stocking a wide variety of items for both. Advice is available from the friendly and helpful staff who are always on hand to answer gardener's questions making Ladds Garden Centre an ideal place for anyone looking to improve or maintain their garden.

WARGRAVE   MAP 2 REF G9
10 miles W of Windsor on the A321

This charming village developed as a settlement in the 10th century at the confluence of the Rivers Thames and Loddon on an area of flat land in a wooded valley. Mentioned in the Domesday Book, when it was referred to as Weregrave, in 1218, the Bishop of Winchester was granted the rights to hold a market here by Henry III. However, this was obviously not a great success as there is no record of a market taking place after the 13th century.

Now an attractive riverside village, the peace was disturbed here in 1914 when suffragettes burnt down the church in protest at the vicar's refusal to remove the word 'obey' from the marriage service. In the churchyard however, undisturbed by the riot, lies the **Hannen Mausoleum**, a splendid monument that was designed for the family by Sir Edwin Lutyens in 1906.

Another interesting sight here can be found on the outskirts of the village, at Park Place. In 1788, the estate was owned by General Henry Conway, Governor of Jersey and, in recognition of his services, the people of the island gave the general a complete **Druids' Temple**. The massive stones were transported from St Helier to the estate and erected in a 25 foot circle in the gardens of his mansion. In 1870, Park Place was destroyed by fire and the estate broken up but today the temple stands in the garden of **Temple Combe**, close to a house designed by the American architect, Frank Lloyd Wright. The only house of his in this country, it was built, in 1958, on an elaborate U-shaped design and has suede panelled walls inside.

HURLEY   MAP 2 REF G8
9 miles NW of Windsor off the A4130

Known to the Danes as Herlie and mentioned in the Domesday Book, this is a picturesque riverside village with delightful walks along the banks and a lock that is well worth the visit. The oldest building here is said to date back to around 1086, the remains of Benedictine monastery are still visible, and the monastic church is still in use. Even **Ye Olde Bell Hotel** is ancient. It is thought to have housed visitors to the monastery, and today it is famous for its food, clientele, and the film stars who are now the frequent visitors.

Found in a delightful, rural, riverside setting, **Hurley Farm Caravan and Camping Park** is a wonderful, peaceful site that was established in 1926. Owned and personally run by brothers David and Richard Burfitt, the park lies on part of the family's 500 acre farm and they also continue to work. Spread over an area of some 15 acres, the park is beautifully landscaped using hedging and trees to provide holiday makers with privacy but not an over-shaded environment. As well as the on-site shop, campers can also enjoy the other modern amenities here which include electric hook-ups, hot water and showers, and a

**Hurley Farm Caravan and Camping Park, Hurley Farm, Hurley,
Berks SL6 5NE Tel: 01628 823501 Fax: 01628 825533**

laundrette. Awarded the David Bellamy Gold Award, the famous naturalist is an occasional visitor here where he is always interested in the conservation and environmental efforts of David and Richard. Plans are afoot to convert one of the farm's barns into a visitor attraction and those staying here are welcome to visit the farm where, at appropriate times, new born lambs can be seen. The park is open from March to October and there are also a limited number of caravan holiday homes for hire here on a weekly basis. The ideal place for a family holiday base, Hurley Farm is well placed for all the local attractions as well as being at the heart of some beautiful countryside.

MAIDENHEAD

6 miles NW of Windsor on the A4130

MAP 2 REF H8

Originally a small settlement along the River Thames, it developed during the Middle Ages, after the construction of a bridge over the Thames in 1280. However, it was as a coaching town, in the 18th century, that saw the town begin to thrive. Ideally situated on the route west, from London to Bath, the town was a convenient place for stopovers. Unfortunately, with thick woods to the west, it was also an excellent place for highwaymen and Dick Turpin is known to have hidden there to rob rich travellers.

Transport has certainly played its part in the town's history for it was the coming of the railways which turned Maidenhead into a fashionable Victorian Thamesside resort. The construction of Isambard Kingdom Brunel's famous **Railway Bridge**, the largest bricked span bridge in the world, completed in 1839 was seen as a pinnacle of engineering achievement.

Meanwhile, on the river, there is the equally famous **Boulter's Lock**, one of the biggest on the Thames, which is today as busy with leisure craft during the summer as it always has been. Boulter is the old word for miller and a flour mill has stood on Boulter's Island since Roman times. Also on the island is **Mill Head House**, the home of the famous broadcaster, Richard Dimbleby, along with his two sons, Jonathan and David, until his death in 1965.

COOKHAM   Map 2 ref H8
6 miles NW of Windsor on the A4094

This pretty, small town, on the banks of the River Thames, was made famous by the artists Sir Stanley Spencer, who used Cookham as the setting for many of his paintings. Born here towards the end of the 19th century, the town's tribute to its most renowned resident is the **Stanley Spencer Gallery**, a permanent exhibition of his work which is housed in the converted Victorian chapel Stanley visited as a child.

The town is also the home of Swan Upping, the annual July ceremony which is over 600 years old when the newly hatched cygnets are gathered and marked. The swans originally came to England as a gift from Queen Beatrice of Cyprus to Richard I and, from then on, they have been highly prized for their decorative feathers and their meat. Today, all swans on the Thames belong to either the Queen or two of the City of London's livery companies - the Vintners and the Dyers. Each bird is taken from the river and marked according to its owner: the Dyers' birds have one mark; the Vintners' two; and the Queen's birds are left unmarked.

Named after the practice of ringing the swans on the River Thames, **The Old Swan Uppers** is a delightful 150-year-old inn that is both attractive and atmospheric. Owned and personally run by James Bunyan, a charming and relaxed host, the inn is a popular place with both locals and visitors alike. With a cosy interior that reflects perfectly the age of the building, this is the ideal place to come to for a quiet drink and to while away a few hours in pleasant company. However, The Old Swan Uppers serves much more than an excellent pint of beer as it has also gained a reputation for the high standard of its cuisine. From

**The Old Swan Uppers, The Pound, Cookham, Berks SL6 9QE
Tel 01628 521324**

bar meals to the full à la carte menu that is served in the conservatory restaurant, there is certainly something here for everyone and all the dishes are made to order from only the freshest of ingredients. Finally, to complete the picture of a wonderful hostelry, there are six comfortable en-suite guest rooms here for visitors who wish to extend their stay overnight. Found in a separate building from the main inn, anyone taking advantage of this accommodation is sure to have a lovely stay.

BRAY   Map 2 ref H9
3 miles NW of Windsor off the A308

This picturesque riverside village is best remembered for the song, *The Vicar of Bray*. A satirical ballard of the 18th century which tells how the vicar, in order to keep his job, changes his politics and religion as a new monarch comes to the throne. Unfortunately, the dates spanned in the amusing song present the village with a problem. There were three, not just one, vicars at Bray between that time. However, it is a charming story that is associated with a charming place.

DORNEY
MAP 2 REF H9

2 miles NW of Windsor off the A308

One of the finest Tudor manor houses in England, **Dorney Court**, just a short walk from the River Thames, has been the home of the Palmer family since 1530. Built in around 1440, it is an enchanting building which also houses some real treasures including early 15th and 16th century oak furniture, beautiful 17th century lacquer furniture, and 400 years of family portraits. It is also

Dorney Court

here that the first pineapple in England was grown in 1665. However, it is one owner who is perhaps remembered above all the others: Sir Roger Palmer was the husband of Charles II's most notorious mistress, Barbara, an intelligent and beautiful woman, Roger was given the title Earl of Castlemaine for his compliance with the affair.

Found on **Dorney Common**, is the traditional English village of **Boveney**, which served as a wharf in the 13th century as timber was being transported from Windsor Forest. The flint and clapboard church of **St Mary Magdalene**, down by the riverside, was the setting for several scenes from Kevin Costner's film *Robin Hood Prince of Thieves*.

4 Southeast Oxfordshire

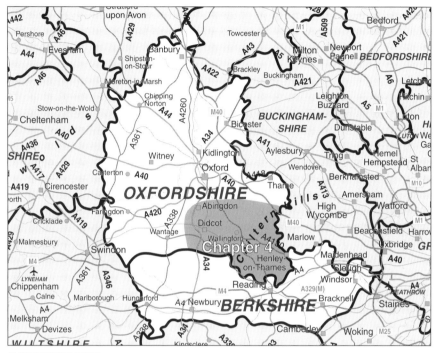

This southeastern corner of Oxfordshire is a place of ancient towns and villages that were well established settlements by the time of the Norman Conquest in 1066. There is the Roman town of Dorchester and the 7th-century abbey town of Abingdon but also a mass of tiny villages and hamlets that are well worth exploring.

Of the best known places here is Henley-on-Thames, famous for its annual Regatta that has drawn people to the riverside for over 150 years. From here the River Thames meanders around Reading to the wonderful old town of Goring, where it makes a turn to the north and enters Oxfordshire entirely. Villages and ancient crossing points line the banks and there are numerous walks along the towpaths which also take in the glorious surrounding countryside. Between Henley and Wallingford, lie the beginnings of the Chiltern Hills, whilst to the north is the beginning of the flat Oxford Plain. A rural landscape with few large towns, this is the ideal area to explore for those who love the English country-side.

HENLEY-ON-THAMES

Reputed to be the oldest settlement in Oxfordshire, this attractive riverside market town has over 300 listed buildings covering several periods. But it is the fine Georgian and Victorian houses and villas fronting on to the River Thames which epitomises the style of Henley-on-Thames.

A quiet and gentle town in 1829 the first inter-varisty boat race, between Oxford and Cambridge, took place here on the river and, within a decade, the event was enjoying royal patronage. Today, Henley's **Regatta**, held every year in the first week of July, is a marvellous and colourful event with teams competing on the mile long course from all over the world. It is also a stylish occasion and is still seen as very much part of the season.

Opened in 1998, the **River and Rowing Museum**, is a fascinating place to visit which traces the rowing heritage of Henley, the river's changing role in the town's history, and there is even the opportunity to 'walk' the length of the River Thames, from source to sea, taking in all the locks. Housed in a spacious, purpose-built building by the award-winning architect, David Chipperfield, visitors can also see the boat in which the British duo, Redgrave and Pinsent, won their gold medal at the 1996 Olympics.

Also situated on the riverbank, beside the town's famous 18th-century bridge, which is appropriately decorated with the faces of Father Thames and the goddess Isis, is the Leander Club, the headquarters of the equally famous rowing club. Whilst on the opposite bank is the attractive Church of St Mary which also acts as a local landmark.

Apart from the boating, which is available throughout the summer, and the pleasant walks along the riverbanks, there are lots of interesting shops, inns, and teashops in the town. Most of the inns are old coaching houses with yards that were once the scene of bull and bear fights.

Just down river from the town centre lies **Fawley Court**, a wonderful private house that was designed by Christopher Wren and built in 1684 for Col W Freeman. Now owned by the Marian Fathers, the **Museum** it contains includes a library, documents relating to the Polish Kings, and memorabilia of the Polish army. The house, gardens, and museum are open to the public from March to October.

To the northwest of Henley lies another interesting house, **Greys Court**, which was rebuilt in the 16th century though it has been added to since. However, it does stand within the walls of the original 14th-century manor house and various of the old outbuildings can still be seen. The property of the National Trust, the gardens of the court contain the **Archbishop's Maze**, which was inspired, in 1980, by Archbishop Runcie's enthronement speech.

Set in the heart of Henley-on-Thames, **Daisy's** is a fascinating shop, owned and run by Sandra O'Halloran, that specialises in everything craft orientated. A

**Daisy's, 45-47 Duke Street, Henley-on-Thames, Oxon RG9 1UR
Tel: 01491 410770**

charming white double-fronted building, with large display windows, Daisy's will appeal to all ages. Ranging from little thimbles to major craft pieces there is certainly something for everyone here: embroidery, china, wooden items, pottery, textiles, and pictures. Attractively displayed, a wander around this well stocked shop is just like delving into Aladdin's Cave. After discovering the wealth of items found here, customers can also take much needed refreshment at the café to the rear of the shop. Serving a mouthwatering range of patisserie along with tea, coffee, and soft drinks, this is the perfect place to take a break after exploring the rest of the shop.

Situated in the town centre, not far from the banks of the River Thames, **The Three Tuns** is a charming old coaching inn that dates from the 16th century. A superb place for a drink and some tasty food, the inn has lost none of its character over the years and many of the original features remain. The low beamed ceilings, the exposed timbers, and the old styled windows all add to the olde

The Three Tuns, 5 Market Place, Henley-on-Thames, Oxon RG9 2AA
Tel: 01491 573260

worlde atmosphere within. As well as serving an excellent range of real ales and beers, including those from the local brewery, The Three Tuns has an enviable reputation for the mouthwatering menu of bar snacks and meals that are available throughout the day. An interesting mix of traditional pub food, there are also some tasty alternatives and a delicious list of desserts that are sure to satisfy those with a sweet tooth. Opening out directly onto the pavement at the front of the pub, to the rear there is a patio area overlooking the lawned garden and its pond. A delightful place to enjoy some refreshment and the peace and quiet offered by this secluded town centre spot.

Frances and Roger Emmett have been at **Little Parmoor Farm** since the early 1970s though this mixed sheep and arable farm has been worked by the

Little Parmoor Farm, Freith, Henley-on-Thames, Oxon RG9 6NL
Tel: 01494 881600 Fax: 01494 883634

family for two generations. At the centre of the farm, in an area of outstanding natural beauty, is the superb 16th-century brick and flint farmhouse from which the couple offer excellent bed and breakfast accommodation in a choice of two guest rooms - one double with en-suite facilities and one twin room with a private bathroom. A typical English large country house, that is stylishly furnished and decorated, this is a comfortable and relaxed place to stay. Surrounding the house is a mature lawned walled garden whilst beyond, there are further grounds with a lovely wooded copse with beech and laurel hedges. From the farmhouse's windows there are views over the garden and the keen eyed will spot pheasants, rabbits, and muntjac deer.

AROUND HENLEY-ON-THAMES

SHIPLAKE
MAP 2 REF F9
2 miles S of Henley-on-Thames on the A4155

It was here, in this small commuter village, that the poet Alfred Tennyson married the local girl, Emily Selwood at St Peter and St Paul's Church. Their engagement had been a long one as Tennyson feared that his family was cursed with melancholia, along with mental and emotional instability, and he did not want to inflict these conditions on his wife or children. The setting for their wedding was indeed a pretty one as the church stands on the river banks and has medieval Belgian glass windows.

The neighbouring village of **Lower Shiplake** can also claim a literary connection as it was the first childhood home of the novelist George Orwell. His family moved here on their return from India and took a house called Roselawn before, after a few years, moving to Henley-on-Thames.

Situated on the banks of the River Thames, **The Baskerville Arms** is a small family run inn that is managed by Derry and Malcolm Hine. Built in the 1930s, originally as a small hotel, the inn was named after the Baskerville family who had land in the area and were also great friends of Conan Doyle, the author of the Sherlock Holmes stories. Recently refurbished, the interior of this imposing

**The Baskerville Arms, Shiplake, near Henley-on-Thames,
Oxon RG9 3NY Tel: 0118 940 3332**

brick building is open plan with plenty of oak panelling and block hardwood floors to add style and warmth. The great mass of decorative pottery and plates which adorn the walls and available nooks and crannies have all been collected by Derry. Food and drink are both, very much, on the menu here and not only is there a great selection of beers, ales, lagers, and wines from the bar but the menu, which ranges from informal snacks and sandwiches to formal à la carte dining, is sure to satisfy all occasions. The large country garden has facilities for children and is popular during the summer, particularly when, weather permitting, barbecues are held there. Finally, The Baskerville Arms also has four spacious and comfortable en-suite guest rooms which makes this an ideal place for all the family to stay.

SONNING COMMON
Map 2 ref F8
3½ miles SW of Henley-on-Thames on the B481

To the southeast of the village lies the **Herb Farm**, where a wide selection of culinary, medicinal, and aromatic herbs are both grown and sold along with old fashioned roses, cottage garden plants, and many wild flowers. However, perhaps the most interesting feature here is the **Saxon Maze**, which was inspired by an illustration of an 8th century mythical Saxon sea creature. Covering an acre of ground, the hedged grass pathways were laid to the unique designs of Adrian Fisher and the maze was opened in 1991. A fascinating experience for all the family, adults have a very definite advantage as the hedges are only five feet high!

MAPLEDURHAM
Map 2 ref E9
6½ miles SW of Henley-on-Thames off the A4074

Found down a small lane which leads to the River Thames, this tiny village is home to Mapledurham House, a Watermill, and a church. The late 16th-century home of the Blount family, **Mapledurham House** was built on the site of an older manor house and it has remained in the same family ever since. As well as viewing the great oak staircase and the fine collection of paintings housed here, visitors will find the house's literary connections are equally interesting: Alexander Pope was a frequent visitor in the 18th century; the final chapters of John Galsworthy's *The Forsythe Saga* were set here; and it was the fictional Toad Hall in *The Wind in the Willows*. However, others may find that the house is familiar as it has also featured in films, such as *The Eagle has Landed*, and television series, including *Inspector Morse*.

Another attraction on the estate is the old riverside **Watermill**, a handsome late 15th-century construction which stands on the site of an earlier building that was mentioned in the Domesday Book. The mill remained in operation until 1947 and it was then the longest surviving working mill on the river. Now fully restored, the traditional machinery can be seen in action grinding wholemeal flour which is then sold through the mill shop.

Whilst in the village the **Church** is also worth a visit as, during restoration work in 1863, the architect, William Butterfield, made great use of coloured brickwork and he also refaced the tower with an bold chequered pattern using flint and brick.

GORING-ON-THAMES
MAP 1 REF E8

9½ miles W of Henley-on-Thames on the B4009

This ancient small town lies across the River Thames from its equally ancient neighbour, Streatly, and, whilst today they are in different counties, they were once in different kingdoms. This is a particularly peaceful stretch of the river, with the bustle of Pangbourne and Henley-on-Thames lying down stream and it is some distance to the towns of Abingdon and Oxford further up stream.

Goring Lock, Goring

However, this has not always been the case as, at one time, the two settlements were often in conflict with each other and excavations in the area have found numerous weapons which date back as far as the Bronze Age.

In the 19th century, after Isambard Kingdom Brunel had laid the tracks for the Great Western Railway through Goring Gap, the village began to grow as it was now accessible to the Thames-loving Victorians. Though there are many Victorian and Edwardian villas and houses here, the original older buildings have survived and they add an air of antiquity to this attractive place.

Found in an idyllic situation **Goring Mill Gallery** is housed in one of the village's oldest buildings. This picturesque and historic watermill dates from the 17th century although it stands on the site of another mill that was re-corded in the Domesday Book. The subject of a painting by Turner in 1805, which also takes in the adjacent Norman church, it is fitting that the building should now be such a splendid gallery. Owned and personally run by Diana Davies and Ron Bridle, the gallery's policy is to exhibit only the work of the very best regional artists and craftsmen in the country. Also in keeping with the age and setting of the building, the works here are generally representational pieces rather than modern or abstract in style.

**Goring Mill Gallery, Lock Approach, Goring-on-Thames, Oxon RG8 9AD
Tel: 01491 875030 Fax: 01491 872519**

On display here are over 500 paintings, ceramics, and sculptures that represent the work of some 50 professional artists and craftspeople. Not surprisingly, the gallery also specialises in landscapes and riverside paintings and, whilst all the works are original pieces, the price range is within the reach of most pockets. In addition to the exceptional display of paintings and craftwork, Goring Mill Gallery also offers customers a wide range of services including commission work, from portraits through to architectural subjects, and a framing service. For anyone who enjoys the English countryside at its best, a visit to Goring Mill Gallery is a must and they will also have an opportunity to take home a unique souvenir of their time by the River Thames.

WOODCOTE   MAP 2 REF E8
7 miles W of Henley-on-Thames off the A4074

To the east of Goring lies the pretty village of Woodcote and, for the very best in French cuisine, **Ricci's on the Green** is the place - a well known restaurant that attracts food lovers from all over the southeast of England. Owned and personally run by Michel Ricci and his wife, Lesley, this superb place has an excellent reputation both locally and within the restaurant trade. Born in the Provencale region of France, where his family own a vineyard, Michel has all the credentials needed to manage this restaurant and it is certainly a delightful and long remembered experience dining here.

Ricci's on the Green, Goring Road, Woodcote, Oxon RG8 0SD
Tel: 01491 680775

The delicious and tantalising menus are produced by Master Chef, John McGeever, the grandson of famous Glasgow chef Maggie Kennedy, who is not only world famous in his own right but also the chairman of the Master Chefs of Great Britain. John believes in producing good food simply and the menus here are a wonderful mix of fresh meat, fish, and vegetables, combined in an interesting and continental manner, that will excite any palate. Whilst the food is certainly superb, the setting in which diners eat is equally well chosen. there are wood block floors, cane backed chairs, and potted palms throughout. The atmosphere of sophistication is enhanced by the discrete lighting, the elegant table settings, and the gentle background music. An exceptional restaurant that is a must for all French food lovers, dining here is a treat well worth travelling to find. Ricci's is open for lunch and dinner from Tuesday to Saturday.

Very much at the centre of village life in Woodcote, **The Red Lion** is a dream come true for Londoner Dennis Smith who, after 20 years in football administration, has always wanted to run a pub in a village with a green. He and his wife, Jean, have been here since 1996 and, in that time, they have certainly made their mark here and in the local community. Appealing to all ages, The Red Lion is very popular with the people of Woodcote as well as being a favourite for walkers and cyclists discovering the local countryside. Built at the turn of the century, the pub has a comfortable and welcoming atmosphere enhanced by the high quality, modern furniture and fittings, the main L-shaped bar is complemented by the non-smoking restaurant extension that will open towards the end of 1999. As well as being a delightful place for a quiet drink, The Red Lion has a comprehensive range of menus that take the customer from lunch-time snacks through to full evening meals and there is also a special Sunday

The Red Lion, Goring Road, Woodcote, near Reading, Berks RG8 0SD
Tel: 01491 680483

lunch menu. Very much a part of the village, not only does the pub have a cricket and a football team but numerous pub games are played here and each Sunday evening Jean and Dennis host a quiz night.

CHECKENDON
MAP 2 REF E8
6 miles W of Henley-on-Thames off the A4074

Situated high in the Chiltern Hills, this small village of timber-framed cottages around a green is many people's idea of the typical English village. To complete the perfect picture, the village church is Norman and, as well as overlooking the green, the interior contains several wall paintings and brasses.

Found deep in rural England, **The Black Horse** has been run by the same family for nearly 100 years and today the pub is managed by Margaret Morgan. A popular place with people from the local area, the pub is also a favourite stopping off point for cyclists and walkers who are taking advantage of the nearby Oxford Cycleway and the Ridgway Walk. Dating back to the 16th century, this wonderful old coaching inn is, as many village pubs were, part of a farm and this is run by Margaret's husband, Martin. Still maintaining a family theme, Margaret's daughter also has a horse livery business running from the farm buildings. In this idyllic setting, visitors to The Black Horse can enjoy warm and friendly hospitality in the quaint old surroundings of this ancient building. The pub comprises three small rooms, end-to-end, and with low ceilings and exposed beams, the place is very cosy indeed, particularly in winter

The Black Horse, Checkendon, Reading, Berks RG8 0TE
Tel: 01491 680418

when the fires are lit. As well as serving customers a superb range of real ales and the usual drinks, Margaret also offers a variety of filled rolls that are all prepared here. For a real country pub that has lost none of its charm over the years, visitors should look no further than The Black Horse.

IPSDEN   MAP 2 REF E8
7½ miles NW of Henley-on-Thames off the A4074

Just south of the village lies the delightful **Wellplace Zoo**, which is home to a whole range of birds and animals. As well as the gentle donkeys, ponies, and other familiar farm animals, the zoo also has monkeys and llamas as well as a magnificent collection of brightly coloured tropical birds. An interesting mix that is sure to keep everyone fascinated and amused.

BENSON   MAP 2 REF E7
9½ miles NW of Henley-on-Thames off the A4130

Though, this century, the village has become associated with the nearby RAF station, it was, in the 18th century, a busy coaching centre and there are still several old coaching inns here to tell the tale. However, some 10 centuries earlier, the village became the home, in AD 777, of King Offa, the ruler of Merica after he had won a victory over the West Saxons. Between 757 and 796, Offa ruled much of southern England as he set about rebuilding the crumbling Mercia kingdom. He was also a Christian ruler and the foundations of the village church date from this period.

EWELME
Map 2 ref E7

9 miles NW of Henley-on-Thames off the B4009

At the centre of this pretty village is a magnificent group of medieval buildings, including the Church, almshouse, and school which were all founded in the 1430s by Alice Chaucer, grand-daughter of the poet Geoffrey, and her husband, the Duke of Suffolk. There is a wonderfully elegant alabaster carving of Alice inside the church and under this effigy is another rather macabre carving of a shrivelled cadaver. In the churchyard is the grave of Jerome K Jerome, author of *Three Men in a Boat*, who moved to the village following the success of his book.

Founded in 1437, the **Almshouses** were built to house 13 poor men and two chaplains were provided to take care of them. They are one of the earliest examples of almshouses built around a quadrangle and they are also one of the earliest brick buildings in the county. The **School** was founded in the same year and it too is of brick though it was extensively altered in Georgian times.

Originally built as three cottages in the 1700s, **Dormer Cottage** is the attractive home of Jean and Bill Standbridge. Since retiring from his milk round, Bill has had much more time to spend with his hobby - miniature railways - and one room of the cottage has been converted to accommodate his superb model railway. Whilst Bill is inside, Jean is outside tending her delightful and typically

Dormer Cottage, High Street, Ewelme, Wallingford, Oxon OX10 6HQ
Tel: 01491 833987

English cottage garden, where she also has an aviary. From their comfortable and interesting home, the couple offer excellent bed and breakfast accommodation in a choice of two well furnished and decorated guest rooms. As with the rest of the cottage, the rooms are cosy and the style of the whole home is warm, welcoming, and very country cottage. A friendly couple who are happy to stop and chat or offer advice to ensure that guests make the most of their stay in the area, Jean also makes sure that no one goes hungry and provides a ruinous breakfast each morning.

WATLINGTON
MAP 2 REF F7

8½ miles NW of Henley-on-Thames on the B4009

To the southeast of the town, itself a charming place with Elizabethan cottages and elegant Georgian houses, lies **Watlington Hill**, one of the high points of the Chiltern Hills. From the top there are superb views over the Oxford plain and the area surrounding the hill is owned by the National Trust.

Found down a quiet country lane whose name derives from gooseberry picking years ago, **West Meadow Bed and Breakfast** is the ideal place for a peaceful few days away. The home of Lindsay and Mike Fear, the cottage stands within its own very English country garden and has views over the adjacent paddocks to the Chiltern Hills beyond, where its now numerous Red Kite population can be seen daily. The attractive and well furnished en-suite guest accommodation is found on the first floor of a converted outbuilding and offers guests not only comfort but also privacy. As well as being elegant and stylish the guest room is also equipped with many of the extras found in only the best hotels. The excellent continental breakfast is brought to the room giving guests an opportunity for a well deserved lie-in.

West Meadow Bed and Breakfast, 28 The Goggs, Watlington, Oxon OX9 5JX Tel: 01491 613278 Fax: 01491 612762

CHRISTMAS COMMON
MAP 2 REF F7
7½ miles NW of Henley-on-Thames off the B4009

This quiet hamlet, surrounded by beech woods, lies in the Chiltern Hills and, as well as the scattered cottages it is also home to a Victorian church.

Dating back to around 1540, **The Fox and Hounds** is a charming and typically English country pub. One of the Civil War landmarks, this is very much a meeting place for the whole village and the council even holds its elections here. As olde worlde inside as it appears from the outside, this is a pub of small

**The Fox and Hounds, Christmas Common, near Watlington,
Oxon OX9 5HL Tel: 01491 612599**

cosy rooms, low ceilings, and an open fire that never goes out. Managed by Freda Gross, as well as being a popular and relaxing place to come to for a quiet pint or two, there is also a lunchtime menu of tasty snacks and sandwiches which always go down well. However, perhaps the most interesting feature of the pub is its darts team - known as the friendliest team in the local league, they never win but certainly know how to enjoy themselves.

STONOR
MAP 2 REF F8
4 miles N of Henley-on-Thames on the B480

The village is the home of Lord and Lady Camoys and their house, **Stonor**, has been in the family for over 800 years. Set in the a wooded valley in the Chilterns and surrounded by a deer park, this attractive house dates from the 12th

Stonor House

century though the beautiful, uniform facade is Tudor and hides much of the earlier work. The interior of the house contains many rare items, including a mass of family portraits, and there is also a medieval Catholic Chapel here that was in continuous use right through the Reformation. In 1581, St Edmund Campion sought refuge at the house and there is an exhibition featuring his life and work. The gardens too are well worth a visit and they offer splendid views over the rolling parkland.

HAMBLEDON   Map 2 ref G8
3 miles NE of Henley-on-Thames off the A4155

The area around Henley-on-Thames has Roman roots there was a Roman villa sited close to the village of Hambleden, just to the north of the town. Set amongst some of the most picturesque Chiltern countryside, **Old Luxters**, also called the Chiltern Valley Winery and Brewery, is one of the most modern

Old Luxters, Hambleden, near Henley-on-Thames, Oxon RG9 6JW
Tel: 01491 638330 Fax: 01491 638645

wineries in Europe. This well established winery produces over 120,000 bottles annually and has achieved over 50 trophies, awards, and commendations in blind-tasted national and international competitions. Old Luxters has also revived the tradition of farm-brewed real ales. The finest malted barleys are brewed to the brewery's own special blend to create a flavour that is packed with depth and rich aroma, so do feel free to sample these delicious brews. Also part of this prestigious establishment is Luxters Gallery which is housed in a large Chiltern barn which has been commended for its restoration in 1990. Exhibitions are held regularly in this opened beamed building, with work supplied from artists of the UK and abroad. There is a wide range of media on display including a unique selection of sculpture and creative furniture. This beautiful gallery also provides an unusual venue for corporate events, conferences, private receptions, and film and photographic location work. In addition to this, David Ealand, the owner of Old Luxters for the last 16 years, hosts regular dinners, wine evenings, tours, and tutored tastings. So those travelling through Hambleden must be sure to drop into Old Luxters and experience first hand the idyllic atmosphere that pervades throughout these old and rustic buildings.

ABINGDON

This is an attractive town and it is also one of the country's oldest as it grew up around a 7th-century Benedictine **Abbey** that was founded here in 675. Sacked twice for its gold and silver when the town was attacked by Danes, the abbey was practically derelict by the 10th century but, under the guidance of Abbot Ethwold, the architect of the great Benedictine reform, it once again prospered and was, in its heyday, larger than Westminster Abbey. Unfortunately little remains today of this great religious house, but the **Gatehouse**, built in the late 15th century, is a splendid reminder. Built on to the abbey gateway is the **Church of St Nicholas**, a much altered building but one which also has managed to retain some of its original Norman features.

The largest town in the Vale of the White Horse, Abingdon was also

Abbey Gatehouse, Abingdon

the county town of Berkshire between 1556 and 1869, indeed, at one time the Abbot here was the second largest landowner in Berkshire after the Crown. This prosperity and importance has given the town an interesting history which can be discovered at the **Abingdon Museum**. Housed in the old **County Hall**, which was originally built as the County Assize Court and Market Hall in 1678, there is plenty to see inside as well as out.

Abingdon Museum

Another of the town's pleasing buildings is the **Church of St Helen**, whose steeple dominates the view southwards along the street. Originally built in the 14th century, the church was remodelled in the 15th and 16th centuries, when the town prospered from a thriving wool trade, to provide an altogether larger and more elaborate building. However, the main glory of the church, the painted ceiling of the Lady Chapel, has been retained from the 14th century.

Beside the churchyard, which contains a curious small building that was the blowing chamber for the church organ, are three sets of almshouses. The oldest, Christ's Hospital, was founded in 1446 whilst the other two, Twitty's Almshouses and Brick Alley Almshouses, date from the early 18th century.

Today, however, Abingdon is perhaps best known for the MG cars, which were built here for 50 years, and the second oldest independent brewery in the country, Morland. Established in the town in 1711, the brewery is famous for its delicious real ales, such as Old Speckled Hen.

AROUND ABINGDON

RADLEY

MAP 1 REF D7

2 miles NE of Abingdon off the A415

This old village is best known for the public school, **Radley College**, housed in the 18th-century Radley Hall, which was founded in 1847. Famous for its rowing, the Radley College Boathouse can be seen along the riverbank. The village **Church of St James** was originally constructed in the 12th century but, in 1290, it was burnt down and rebuilt under the orders of the Abbot of Abingdon. Above the modern pulpit is a carved wooden canopy which once stood over the Speaker's chair in the House of Commons and was given to the church in 1653.

NUNEHAM COURTENAY   MAP 1 REF D7
3½ miles NE of Abingdon on the A4074

When the 1st Earl of Harcourt moved his family here from Stanton Harcourt in 1756, he built the splendid **Nuneham Park**, a Palladian mansion, and had Capability Brown landscape the surrounding parkland. So that the views from the Park would not be interrupted the by the village, the earl had it rebuilt, a mile up from the Thames and, as a result, Nuneham Courtenay is a charming model village of 18th-century cottages. Today, the mansion house is now a conference centre but the village remains a charming place with the cottages still facing each other in matched pairs on either side of the road. The parkland of the house now forms the **Arboretum** of Oxford University and it is open to the public. The 55 acres of woodland and meadow contain many rare species of tree and, with its walks and ponds it is a pleasant place for an afternoon stroll.

CHINNOR   MAP 2 REF F6
15½ miles E of Abingdon on the B4009

A relatively large and bustling village by comparison with the surrounding quiet hamlets and small settlements that make up this area of Oxfordshire. To the east of Chinnor, and reached by a footpath, is **Bledlow Ridge** with its magnificent wooded hillside.

Right in the heart of the village lies **The Red Lion Pub**, an attractive 16th-century building which still retains its barn and which also has a pleasant beer

The Red Lion Pub, 3 High Street, Chinnor, Oxon OX9 4DL
Tel: 01844 351494

garden for customers to use on a sunny day. Very much a locals pub the inn has also played host to Oliver Cromwell who, despite his high moral talk, is said to have had a mistress in the village. As befits a building of this age, the pub has low ceilings, plenty of old oak beams, stone flagged floors, and a real open fire in the winter. Managed by Lynne Malvin and her husband Stephen, this delightful place has two bars where their range of real ales are served - the more rustic of the bars doubles as the games room where dominoes and Aunt Sally are played regularly. Food too is important at The Red Lion and as well as the select menu of tasty dishes there are always several daily specials from which to choose and the traditional Sunday roast lunches are popular. Finally, the inn is also home to a lady ghost who only appears when Lynne is away and, during these times, keys left lying around go missing and the television is switched on and off.

SHILLINGFORD   MAP 1 REF E7
6½ miles SE of Abingdon on the A4074

This typical Thames Valley village is where the Irish poet, WB Yeats, lived with his wife and child in the summer of 1921 while Civil War was raging in Ireland. While here, he began writing the series of poems which he went on to describe as *"a lamentation over lost peace and hope."*

Bordering the River Thames and surrounded by its own farmland, **North Farm** is owned and worked by Hilary and Paul Warburton. At the centre of this mixed arable and sheep farm lies the attractive 18th-century farmhouse, a quiet family home, from which Hilary and Paul offer excellent bed and breakfast accommodation. There is a choice of three well furnished guest rooms, all of which enjoy glorious views over the surrounding countryside, and, as the situation is so peaceful, guests are sure to have a refreshing night's sleep. A traditional

North Farm, Shillingford Hill, Wallingford, Oxon OX10 8NB
Tel: 01865 858406 Fax: 01865 858519

English or Continental breakfast is served each morning which will set anyone up for a full day exploring the area and, for the energetic, there is a hard tennis court at the farm though those wanting a more relaxing time will enjoy the large, well tended garden. The farm also incorporates some mature woodland, ideal for a gentle stroll, and the pet pygmy goats and hens, along with the dogs and cat, are always ready to make friends with the guests.

WARBOROUGH
Map 1 ref E7

6 miles SE of Abingdon on the A329

Set well back from the main road through the village there is a large cricket pitch around which can be found several attractive buildings, including a large, thatched barn. A rural village, the ploughing competition held here is said to take place in the biggest field in England.

The Cricketers Arms, in the heart of the village, is a wonderful old 17th-century coaching inn that is everything an English country pub should be. Managed since 1998 by Lynne and John Piggott, a professional couple with

The Cricketers Arms, Thame Road, Warborough, Oxon OX10 7DD
Tel: 01865 858192

three grown up children, this delightful place is not only popular with the local people but a welcome stopping point for anyone visiting the area. As well as the attractive beer garden, complete with safe play area, the interior of the pub provides a quiet and relaxing atmosphere where customers can enjoy the superb hospitality that is on offer. Charmingly decorated, stylishly furnished, and with a wide variety of personal knickknacks on display, this is not just the pub to come to for real ale but a delicious menu of tasty home-cooked food is served either in the bar or in the intimate dining room. However, this is not all The Cricketers Arms has to offer as there are also three comfortable guest rooms that have all been newly furnished and fitted in 1999.

DORCHESTER   Map 1 ref E7
5 miles SE of Abingdon off the A4074

This small town, situated on the River Thames and just a short walk from the River Thames, was once an important Roman station called Dorocina. The name comes from the Celtic word, Dor, and the Roman word, Chester and it was here that Christianity was established in the southwest of England by St Birinus. Known as the Apostle of the West Saxons, Birinus was consecrated in Genoa, landed in Wessex in 634, and converted King Cynegils of Wessex the following year. In gratitude, the king gave Dorchester to Birinus and it became a centre of missionary activity.

The **Abbey Church of St Peter and St Paul** is all that remains of the Augustinian Abbey which was built on the site of the original Saxon Church in 1170. Its chief glory is the 14th-century choir and the huge 'Jesse' window, showing the family tree of Jesus, which has retained its original glass. The story of the

Abbey Museum, Dorchester

abbey, along with the history of settlement in the area going back to neolithic times, is told in the **Abbey Museum** which is housed in a former Grammar Schoolroom, built in 1652.

In the 18th-century the High Street would have been a busy thoroughfare but it has now been by-passed which has had the effect of turning the street into a peaceful backwater and the attractive houses can be viewed at leisure.

LITTLE WITTENHAM   Map 1 ref D7
4½ miles SE of Abingdon off the A4130

Lying beneath the **Wittenham Clumps**, which, for centuries, were an important defensive position overlooking the Thames crossing at Dorchester and are now a nature reserve, this secluded village has a number of pretty cottages. Down towards the river lies another of the village's charms, St Peter's Church, which contains the effigies of Sir William Dunch, a former MP for Wallingford, and his wife, the aunt of Oliver Cromwell.

Just to the northwest, towards the village of Long Wittenham, lies **Pendon Museum**, founded by Roye England, an Australian who came to study in England in 1925. As he took up his studies, England was horrified to see ancient buildings being pulled apart or knocked down completely to make way for modern, characterless buildings and extensions. Seeking a way to preserve the past, England set about recreating the best of the countryside and its buildings in model form and the museum, which includes his model railways (another passion), is a tribute to his hard work.

Found to the southeast, above the Little Wittenham, is **Sinodun Hill**, which was originally the site of a powerful Iron Age fort. It was also used by the Romans as a camp because of its commanding views of the area.

WALLINGFORD   Map 1 ref E8
8 miles SE of Abingdon on the A4130

This ancient town has been a crossing point of the River Thames since prehistoric times and, because of this, it has also been a strategic place. Alfred the Great first fortified the town, against the Danes, and the Saxon earth defences can still be seen. It was here that William the Conqueror, after the Battle of Hastings, crossed the river on his six-day march to London. He also saw the strategic importance of the town and, under his instruction, a castle was built here though, today, only parts of the walls remain.

Wallingford was also an important trading town: it received its charter in 1155 and it had its own mint for several centuries. Queen Matilda made this her base after she had been ousted from the throne and, to avoid capture, she fled across the frozen river.

During the Civil War Wallingford aligned itself to the Royalist cause whose headquarters were at nearby Oxford. However, in 1646, the town walls were destroyed and Wallingford surrendered to General Fairfax, leader of Cromwell's army. The **Museum of Local History**, in the High Street, tells the interesting story of this old settlement .

On the other side of the river lies **Howbery Park Institute of Hydrology** that the was once the home of Jethro Tull in the early 18th century. It was here that Tull developed the horse-drawn seed drill and other innovations that earned him the title, Father of modern farming.

BLEWBURY   MAP 1 REF D8
7 miles S of Abingdon on the A417

Found in the foothills of the Berkshire Downs, this beautiful village is full of attractive thatched and timber-framed houses. During the 19th century, Blewbury became a Mecca for artists and writers wishing to practice their work in the peaceful surroundings and it remains very much the same today. The Tudor-brick house in which Kenneth Grahame, author of *The Wind in the Willows*, lived from 1910 to 1924 is also still to be seen here.

DIDCOT   MAP 1 REF D7
4½ miles S of Abingdon on the A4130

The giant cooling towers of Didcot's power station dominate the skyline for miles around and there is little left to be found of the old town. However, the saving grace is the **Didcot Railway Centre**, a shrine to the days of the steam engine and the Great Western Railway. Isambard Kingdom Brunel designed the Great Western Railway and its route through Didcot, from London to Bristol, was completed in 1841. Until 1892 its trains ran on their unique broad gauge tracks and the GWR retained its independence until the nationalisation of the railways in 1948. Based around the engine shed, where visitors can inspect the collection of steam locomotives, members of the Great Western Society have recreated the golden age of the railway at the centre which also includes a beautiful recreation of a country station, complete with level crossing. Steam days are held through out the year when locomotives once again take to the broad gauge track and visitors can also take in the Victorian signalling system and the centre's Relics Display.

MILTON   MAP 1 REF D7
2½ miles S of Abingdon off the A4130

The delightful **Milton Manor House**, designed by Inigo Jones, is an extraordinarily beautiful 18th-century gentleman's residence. Developed for Bryant Barrett, King George III's lacemaker, from a small country manor house built in 1663, it is still lived in by the family and remains one of Oxfordshire's finest manors. Of particular interest to those who take advantage of its summer opening times, is the celebrated Strawberry Hill Gothic Library and the attractive

Catholic chapel. Set in glorious parkland with a pretty walled garden, two lakes, and stables, this meticulously restored house is well worth visiting.

SUTTON COURTENAY   MAP 1 REF D7
2 miles S of Abingdon on the B4016

A pretty village that was mentioned in the Domesday Book, the abbey here, first founded in 1350, is now a small community of both men and women who concentrate on personal and spiritual growth.

The village **Church of All Saints**, which dates back to Norman times, houses some fine stone carvings and woodwork but the real interest lies in the churchyard. Here can be found the grave of Herbert Asquith, the last Liberal Prime Minister (from 1908 to 1916) and also the grave of Eric Blair. Better known as novelist George Orwell, there are several yew trees planted here in his memory.

5 West Oxfordshire

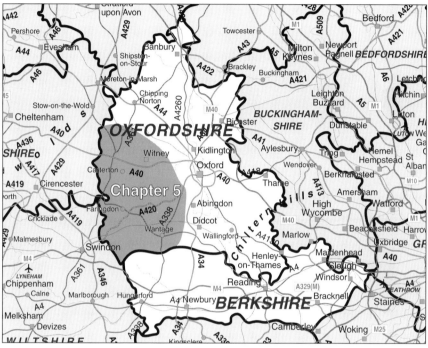

© MAPS IN MINUTES ™ (1998)

West Oxfordshire is a region of several different landscapes. There are the Berkshire Downs marking the southern border, with the Vale of the White Horse, the River Thames cuts the area in two, and to the north are the beginnings of the Cotswolds. A rural region, of ancient towns and villages, this is an excellent place that well deserves exploring.

Wantage, the birthplace of Alfred the Great, lies on the edge of the downs and the old town makes a sensible starting point as it is also home to the Vale and Downland Museum Centre. The region's most famous feature, the White Horse, lies away to the west, to the south of Uffington. Here, the edge of the downlands are littered with Iron Age hill forts and other relics and it is also the line of the famous Ridgeway footpath. Over 80 miles in length, the footpath, which starts near Avebury and finishes at Ivinghoe Beacon, near Tring, follows the route of a prehistoric track.

Further north, on the other side of the River Thames, is the old town of Witney, famous for its blankets, which, by contrast is a Cotswold settlement. A pleasant and interesting place to spend some time, anyone travelling to the town from the south will hardly fail to notice the abundance of ancient manor houses and churches which lie scattered throughout the landscape.

WANTAGE

This thriving market town was, in 849, the birthplace of Alfred the Great and Wantage remained a Royal Manor until end of the 12th century. In the central market place, around which there are some fine Georgian and Victorian buildings, is a huge statue of the King of the West Saxons, who spent much of his life (he died in 899) defending his kingdom from the Danes in the north before becoming the overlord of England. An educated man for his time, as a boy Alfred had visited Rome, he not only codified the laws of his kingdom bur also revived learning.

Unfortunately, only the **Church of St Peter and St Paul** has survived from medieval times and, though much restored in 1857 by GE Street, there are various features that have remained from the original 13th-century structure and visitors can also see a brass commemorating the life of Sir Ivo Fitzwarren, the father of Dick Whittington's wife, Alice.

Opposite the church is the **Vale and Downland Museum Centre**, which is found in another of the town's old buildings - a house dating from the 16th century - and a reconstructed barn. Dedicated to the geology, history, and archaeology of Wantage and the Vale of the White Horse, the displays cover the centuries from prehistoric times to the present day.

Built as the home of the Wantage Sisterhood, an Anglican Order, in the 19th century, three architects were involved in the construction of **St Mary's Convent**: GE Street; William Butterfield, architect of Keble College, Oxford; and John Pearson, architect of Truro Cathedral.

Just to the east of the town lies **Ardington House**, a beautifully symmetrical, early 18th-century building that is the home of the Baring family. Occasionally open to the public, the best feature here is the Imperial Staircase - where two flights come into one - of which this is a particularly fine example.

Situated on the main road through the town, **The Volunteer** is a charming old inn managed by Ian and Jackie Crayford. Their philosophy is to open eight days a week if customers want serving and the couple certainly aim to ensure that all their customers leave the inn well and truly satisfied. As one of the Hook Norton Brewery chain, the inn, naturally, serves an excellent range of the brewery's real ales but Ian, an experienced butcher, and Jackie have also put the inn on the map as a place for superb food. Famous for the all day breakfast, the menu of simple and traditional pub food is well worth making the trip to try.

The Volunteer, Station Road, Wantage, Oxon OX12 0DH
Tel: 01235 769557

As well as having an attractive beer garden, where summer barbecues are held, there is a secure and safe children's play area and also an Aunt Sally alley. The interior of the pub is equally attractive and, with plenty of comfortable seating, it is the ideal place to stop and relax over a drink and a meal. Tastefully decorated, there are numerous pictures and cartoons of pigs on the walls and Jackie's collection of miniature porcelain pigs is also on display. A while ago, one of the pigs went missing and the couple received postcards from all over the world - supposedly from the wandering pig. Eventually, it returned home, in a taxi from Witney station, but to this day no one knows exactly who the abductor was. Just in case good food and drink and missing pigs is not enough to attract visitors, The Volunteer also has two delightful en-suite guest rooms which make this an ideal place to stay whilst in the area.

AROUND WANTAGE

WEST HANNEY   MAP 1 REF C7
2½ miles N of Wantage off the A338

Now divided into three, the village green here once stretched from the parish church, in the south, to the Old Pond. Found on Main Green, the village's old medieval **Buttercross**, which looks rather like a market cross, is all that remains of a structure (of several supporting pillars with a roof) under which traders sold their wares.

St James' Church, beside which stands Prior's Court, a Jacobean house that was the manor of West Hanney, occupies a Saxon site and the building itself dates from the 12th century. Inside, can be found a tablet to Elizabeth Bowles who died in 1718 at the alleged age of 124 years. Though it is impossible to verify this claim, she is the longest lived Englishwoman recorded.

KINGSTON BAGPUIZE   MAP 1 REF C7

6 miles N of Wantage off the A420

This straddling village's intriguing name dates back to Norman times when Ralf de Bachepuise, a contemporary of William the Conqueror, was given land in the area. The village grew to serve the estate of Kingston Bagpuize House and many of the buildings, including the church and village school dates from the 18th century.

Kingston Bagpuize House is the home of Francis and Virginia Grant and their two young children, Elizabeth and Alexander. Though the manor of Kingston was in existence before the Norman Conquest, much of the documentary evidence regarding the origins of the manor house were lost before World War II. However, it is known that a 16th-century moated farmhouse was still standing when the present house was built in the 1660s though both the exterior and the interior were extensively remodelled in the early 1700s. Visitors to the house, which remains very much a family home, will see, among the treasures, the magnificent cantilevered staircase and gallery, the elegant drawing rooms with its twin 18th-century fireplaces, and the panelled library and dining room.

Kingston Bagpuize House and Gardens, Kingston Bagpuize, near Abingdon, Oxon OX13 5AX Tel: 01865 820259 Fax: 01865 821659

However, it is the gardens which bring many visitors to the house. Showing traces of much earlier gardens, the grounds contain a large collection of trees, shrubs, and perennials, including some rare and unusual species. Some of the yews are over 300 years old and there are handsome Wellingtonias planted in the last century. The greatest influence on the present garden was Miss Marlie Raphael, Great Aunt of Francis Grant, and owner of the house from 1939 until her death in 1976. In the 1950s and 1960s she planted extensively including the creation of her woodland garden with the aim of giving colour and interest throughout the year. She was advised by Sir Harold Hillier from whose nurseries the majority of her plants came. Along with restoring the gardens to their former glory, Virginia and Francis have also spent time in identifying many of the plants found here and their garden map is sure to add to visitors' enjoyment.

On all open days teas with a selection of home-made cakes, scones, and biscuits are available in the tea room which is in the original basement kitchen of the house. For pre-booked group visits morning coffee and light lunches are also available. The house and gardens are open on specific days from March to October and, at all other times for group visits by written appointment.

LONGWORTH
MAP 1 REF C7

6½ miles N of Wantage off the A420

Looking every inch a typical Cotswold village, Longworth lies just a short walk from the banks of the River Thames, which lies to the north. One of the rectors of the pretty 13th-century St Mary's Church, was the father of Richard Doddridge Blackmore, the author of *Lorna Doone*.

APPLETON
MAP 1 REF C6

8½ miles NE of Wantage off the A420

This attractive village of pretty thatched cottages surrounding the duck pond is also home to a moated manor house which contains both Norman and Tudor architecture.

The Thatched Tavern, which has never had a thatched roof, is a charming 16th-century building that was converted into a pub some 200 years ago after being handed over by the Lord of the Manor for the benefit of the local thatchers. Today, the patrons of this warm and friendly inn come from many different walks of life but all benefit from the excellent hospitality offered by today's licensees Chris and Susanne Prothero. Cosy and full of olde worlde charm inside, this is a pub with very low ceilings so taller customers beware. As well as being well known locally for the delicious real ales that are on tap behind the bar, The Thatched Tavern also offers customers a tasty menu of snacks and meals at both lunchtime and in the evening from Tuesday to Sunday.

A much used meeting place for the people of Appleton, this is not only a place to come to take refreshment and catch up on the gossip but also to enjoy a game

The Thatched Tavern, Appleton, Oxon OX13 5JH
Tel: 01865 864814

or two. As well as more usual pub games of darts, cribbage, Aunt Sally, and bar skittles, Austrian Nailing is very popular. An obscure game where six inch nails are hammered into a huge tree trunk with the opposite end of a brick hammer, it is thought that the game originated from the mountains and mimics the hammering of spikes into the ice face. As with most pub games, Austrian Nailing becomes progressively harder as the evening wears on!

GARFORD   Map 1 ref C7
5 miles NE of Wantage off the A338

Though there is little to see here now, excavations have revealed that the village was inhabited during the Iron Age and the earliest structures unearthed are timber-built round huts with pits for storing grain. Towards the end of pre-historic times a shrine was also built here and, with the coming of the Romans, the site seems to have kept its religious significance - a Romano Celtic temple was built at the end of the 1st century AD. A sizeable building for the time, with sides 25 feet long, a stone-built circular structure was also erected just to the south of the temple. Though its use is unknown this was clearly an important centre of worship

Venn Watermill, Garford

over a long period of time - the site seems to have been used for religious purposes well into the 5th century.

To the south of the village, on a tributary of the River Thames, lies **Venn Watermill**. Complete with its machinery and waterwheel, the mill dates from the late 18th century and is open by appointment.

STEVENTON
MAP 1 REF C7

5 miles NE of Wantage on the A4185

Found along a tree-lined road **Priory Cottages** were converted from former monastic buildings and they are now owned by the National Trust. One of the cottages contains the original Great Hall of Priory and it is only the hall that is open to the public throughout the summer months.

HARWELL
MAP 1 REF D8

6 miles E of Wantage on the A417

An ancient village of timber-framed cottages, with a Norman church and some fine almshouses, Harwell is best known for the Atomic Energy Research Establishment that was founded here in 1946. Lying to the south of the original village, this nuclear research centre almost forms a village in its own right.

EAST HENDRED
MAP 1 REF C8

4 miles E of Wantage off the A417

Situated on the edge of the rolling Berkshire Downs, this is one of Oxfordshire's prettiest villages, with its half-timbered 16th- and 17th-century cottages and thatched cob walls. Next door to the 14th-century priests' house lies Champs Chapel which is now home to the village **Museum**, which tells the story of this once thriving market town. Visitors to East Hendred can also take in the attractive St Augustine's Church, with its impressive tower dating from 1450, and Hundred House, home of the Eyston family, who were descendants of Sir Thomas More.

LETCOMBE BASSETT
MAP 1 REF C8

2 miles S of Wantage off the B4001

This tiny village has a notable place in literary history: it is called Cresscombe in *Jude the Obscure*, which Thomas Hardy wrote whilst staying here. Earlier, Jonathan Swift spent the summer of 1714 at the village's rectory where he was visited by the poet Alexander Pope.

Just to the east of the village lies **Segsbury Camp**, which is sometimes also referred to as **Letcombe Castle**. Set on the edge of the Berkshire Downs, this massive Iron Age hill fort encloses some 26 acres of land.

EAST AND WEST CHALLOW
MAP 1 REF C8/B8

1 mile W of Wantage on the A417

The village church in the seemingly modern village of **East Challow** dates from the 12th century but, in the mid 19th century it underwent a major reconstruction and the two Norman doorways were lost. Just a quarter of a mile to the west lie the small group of houses and farms of **West Challow** and another loss was the closing of the Wiltshire and Berkshire Canal, in 1914, which passed through the village during the 19th century.

Situated in the heart of farming country, **Coppice Leaze Farm** is the charming Georgian home of Sas Hickman and her family. A teacher of dyslexic children, Sas also offers comfortable bed and breakfast accommodation from this delight-

Coppice Leaze Farm, West Challow, near Wantage, Oxon OX12 9TJ
Tel: 01235 765080 Fax: 01235 760475

ful family house. Well decorated and furnished, there are two individually coordinated guest rooms which each have a share of the guest bathroom. A traditional home-cooked breakfast is served each morning and guests are free to enjoy not only the surrounding countryside but the house's mature walled garden, the pond, and the abundant wildlife.

KINGSTON LISLE
MAP 1 REF B8

4½ miles W of Wantage off the B4507

Just to the southwest of the attractive Norman Church of St John lies the **Blowing Stone** (or **Sarsen Stone**), a piece of glacial debris that is perforated with holes. When blown, the stone emits a fog-horn like sound and tradition has it that the stone was blown by King Alfred.

Also found here, on the edge of the downs, is **Kingston Lisle Park**, which was built in 1677 and later enlarged in the early 1800s. Once the home of Mary Anne Hughes, a great expert on local folklore, she was also a friend of Sir Walter Scott, Charles Dickens, and the Victorian writer of historical novels, Harrison Ainsworth. Ainsworth is known to have stayed at the house on many occasions and he dedicated his novel, *Guy Fawkes*, published in 1841, to Mrs Hughes. The house and park remain in private hands and are not open to the public.

The Blowing Stone Inn, in the heart of Kingston Lisle, is named after the stone that King Alfred blew to summon his troops and the famous stone can still be seen here. Surrounded by rolling countryside in all directions, the inn, which has been owned and personally run by Mr and Mrs Snelson since 1994, is the ideal place for anyone looking for some delicious refreshment whilst in the area.

**The Blowing Stone Inn, Kingston Lisle, Near Wantage, Oxon OX12 9QX
Tel: 01367 820288**

Well known for its shooting parties, this 1930s pub is well used to catering to the needs of those who have worked up an appetite and, as well as an excellent pint of beer available, the well chosen menu is sure to satisfy the hungriest of outdoor types. A comfortable and pleasant place in which to relax, The Blowing Stone is well furnished and stylishly decorated, and the tables in the conservatory dining room are beautifully laid with linen napkins, crystal glassware, and fresh flowers. Those looking for overnight accommodation are also in for a treat as there are five guest rooms at the inn which all live up to the high standards set by the rest of the inn.

UFFINGTON
MAP 1 REF B8

5½ miles W of Wantage off the B4507

This large village was, in 1822, the birthplace of Thomas Hughes, the son of the vicar and grandson of Mary Anne Hughes of Kingston Lisle. The author of *Tom Brown's Schooldays*, Hughes incorporates many local landmarks, including the White Horse and Uffington Castle, in his well known work. The **Tom Brown's School Museum** tells the story of Hughes' life and works.

Tom Brown's School Museum, Uffington

However, the village is perhaps best known for the **Uffington White Horse**, where on the hillside a mysteriously abstract and very beautiful figure of a horse, some 400 feet long, has been created by removing the turf to expose the gleaming white chalk beneath. It is a startling sight which can be seen from far and wide, and many a tantalising glimpse of it has been caught through the window of a train travelling through the valley below. Popular tradition links it with the victory of King Alfred over the Danes at the battle of Ashdown, which was fought somewhere on these downs in 871, but modern thinking now considers that it dates from about 100 BC.

Above the White Horse is the Iron Age camp known as **Uffington Castle**, and to one side is a knoll known as **Dragon's Hill** where legend has it that St George killed the dragon.

COMPTON BEAUCHAMP
MAP 1 REF B8

7 miles W of Wantage off the B4507

The pretty parish **Church of St Swithin** is built of chalk, presumably from the local downs, and its key features are the medieval glass and the Victorian wall paintings. St Swithin is an unusual dedication and it was perhaps made here as St Swithin was the Bishop of Winchester in the late 9th century and therefore something of a local boy.

ASHBURY
MAP 1 REF A8

8 miles W of Wantage on the B4000

To the southeast of this village on the edge of the Berkshire Downs lies **Wayland's Smithy**, a prehistoric burial place and, originally, a long mound of earth that would have covered a stone chamber. Today, the stones, of a local sandstone known as sarsen, are exposed and they stand in a small wood. Built about 2000 BC, Wayland was the smith of the gods and he figured in a number of Teutonic and Norse myths, fashioning powerful swords or beautiful jewels according to the needs of the story. Sir Walter Scott made great use of the local legend - anyone leaving their horse and a coin at the Smithy could return to find it shod by Wayland - in his novel *Kenilworth*.

GREAT COXWELL
8 miles NW of Wantage off the A420

MAP 1 REF B7

This village is well known for its magnificent 13th-century **Tithe Barn** and its **Church of St Giles**, which also dates from that time. A simple and elegant building, the church is often overlooked in favour of the barn which was originally built to serve the needs of the Cistercian Abbey at Beaulieu in Hampshire who were granted the land here by King John. An impressive building that is some 152 feet long, with Cotswold stone walls of over four feet thick, this huge barn was used to store the tithe - or taxes - received from the tenants of the church land. At the Dissolution it passed into private ownership and, today, it is owned by the National Trust.

BUSCOT
11 miles NW of Wantage on the A417

MAP 1 REF A7

This small village, in the valley of the upper Thames, is home to two National Trust properties: **Buscot Old Parsonage** and **Buscot Park**. The parsonage is a lovely house, with a small garden on the banks of the River Thames, that was built of Cotswold stone in 1703. However, Buscot Park is a much grander affair, as its name might suggest, and this classic example of a late Georgian house was built in 1780. Home of the Faringdon Art Collection, which includes paintings by Rembrandt, Murillo, and Reynolds, there is one room here that is decorated with a series of pictures painted by Edward Burne-Jones, the pre-Raphaelite artist who was a close friend of William Morris. Painted in 1890, they reflect Burne-Jones' interest in myths and legends and they tell the story of the Sleeping Beauty.

Anyone particularly interested in the work of Burne-Jones should also visit the village church, where a stained glass window showing the Good Shepherd was designed by him in 1891, when he was working with William Morris's firm, Morris and Co. The church itself is very nicely situated, by the river just outside the village.

FARINGDON
8 miles NW of Wantage on the A417

MAP 1 REF B7

This pleasant market town, with its old market hall and some picturesque inns, takes its name from the Old English for Fern Hill. The town's **Church of All Saints**, prominently placed overlooking the market place, is a large cross-shaped building which has developed, over the years, from the original Norman core. At one time the church had a steeple but this was destroyed during the Civil War although the ironwork on the main door has remained in tact for over 700 years.

To the west of the church is the beautiful 18th-century **Faringdon House**, built by George III's poet laureate, Henry James Pye. Ridiculed by the rest of the literary scene of the time, Pye was also forced to sell the house after becoming a Member of Parliament as he had run up excessive election expenses.

The house has other literary associations and one in particular comes from a more chilling time the history of the family, who had lived in an earlier house on the same site. Legend has it that the headless ghost of Hampden Pye haunts the grounds. He was serving in the Navy as a midshipman when his stepmother, who wanted her own son to inherit the estate, plotted with his captain to make sure he did not return to England alive. Hampden was indeed killed in action at sea, though this does not seem to have been as a result of his stepmother's plot, and his ghost returned to haunt her. This story was told to Richard Harris Barham by Mary Hughes and Barham used it in one of his Ingoldsby Legends under the name of *The Legend of Hamilton Tighe*.

Finally, in the 1930s, the house became the property of Lord Berners and it was he who built the **Folly** on Faringdon Hill in 1935. Probably the last folly of any size to be built in this country, this 140 foot high brick tower has an arcaded lookout room and culminates in a Gothic lantern tower.

FERNHAM Map 1 ref B7
7 miles NW of Wantage off the A417

The attractive 17th-century **Woodman Inn** lies very much at the heart of village

The Woodman Inn, Fernham, near Faringdon, Oxon SN7 7NZ
Tel: 01367 820643

life in Fernham, which lies just south of Faringdon. Though, unfortunately, many of the papers that contained the licensing grants were destroyed by a fire at Reading in 1703, the earliest recorded landlord was William King in 1840 whilst the longest serving was James Warner and his family from 1915 to 1971. However, the best remembered landlord is sure to be John Lane who bought the pub in 1971. Since then The Woodman Inn has seen many changes for the better and Daphne, John's wife, is carrying with his legacy following his untimely death in the spring of 1999. Popular with both locals and those visiting the Vale of the White Horse, the inn has a delightful open plan bar area that retains the exposed beams, small windows, and low ceilings of the original building. The walls are decorated with old farming implements and, in a central position, is a warming open fire with a skillet and boiling pot still.

Well known far and wide for the high standard and excellent quality of its real ale, the food served at The Woodman Inn is equally enjoyable. Certainly a cut above the normal pub food, the menu includes many favourites but also more interesting and unusual dishes such as kangaroo and wild boar feature regularly. Adjacent to the bar is a wonderful medieval banqueting hall complete with benches, settles, and window seats. Dining by candle light, banqueters can enjoy a delicious meal with a real Middle Ages ambience.

CHARNEY BASSETT
4 miles N of Wantage off the B4508

MAP 1 REF C7

This typical Vale of the White Horse village comprises pretty stone and thatched cottages surrounding the central green. As well as the restored watermill on the banks of the River Ock and the small but charming Church of St Peter, with its Norman carvings and Jacobean bellcote, there also lies, just a short walk away, the Iron Age hill fort of **Cherbury Camp**. Constructed on an easily defensible position, this is the only multivallante hill fort in the county.

WITNEY

Situated at the bottom of the valley of the River Windrush, this old town's name is derived from Witta's Island and it was once of importance as the Wittan, the Council of the Saxon Kings, met here. Developed as a planned town in the early Middle Ages, under the guidance of the Bishop of Winchester, the site of the Bishop's Palace lies alongside **St Mary's Church**. With an attractive exterior, though the interior does not live up to the promise, the church provides a dramatic focus to the town's market place. By 1278, Witney had a weekly market and two annual fairs and in the centre of the market place still stands the **Buttercross**. Originally a shrine, the cross has a steep roof with rustic-looking stone columns and it was probably built in 1600.

Witney Buttercross

Wool was the economic base of life here and Witney developed weaving and, in particular, the making of blankets. The Witney Blanket Company was incorporated in 1710 but before that there were over 150 looms here working in the blanket trade employing over 3000 people. The **Blanket Hall**, in the High Street, has on it the arms of the Witney Company of Weavers and it was built for the weighing and measuring of blankets in an age before rigid standardisation. The trade began in the 16th century and, even though there has been a great decline in the industry since World War I, there are sill a couple of blanket factories here.

Just outside the town is the **Cogges Manor Farm Museum**, which stands on the site of a now deserted medieval village of which only the church, priory, and manor house remain. A museum of farming and country life, the displays tell the story of the lives of those who have worked the surrounding land over the centuries.

Found in the heart of Witney is one of the area's premier antiques businesses, **Witney Antiques**. Highly regarded in the world of antiques and collectibles, and with a worldwide reputation, these magnificent showrooms are owned and run by Mr and Mrs Stephen Jarrett. The excellent collection of fine furniture is displayed in a series of rooms, each of which is given over to a different century - from the oak and walnut of the 17th and 18th centuries to the mahogany of the 18th and early 19th centuries. As well as concentrating on superb examples of English furniture, Witney Antiques also has a substantial collection of antiques from Europe all of which, like the furniture, is presented in a attractive manner.

However, what makes Witney Antiques exceptional are the two areas in which

Witney Antiques, 96-100 Corn Street, Witney, Oxon OX8 7BU
Tel: 01993 703902 Fax: 01993 779852

it specialises. Firstly, there is a department devoted to clocks and timepieces - from traditional English long case clocks to ornate French table clocks. Finally, there is a magnificent collection of 17th-century needlework and 18th and 19th-century samplers for sale which is thought to be the largest in the country. Mrs Jarrett's interest in samplers began as a hobby and, over the years, whilst she has become very much a specialist in this area, Witney Antiques has also become a centre for textile collectors. Those visitors who are particularly interested in textiles should take note that Witney Antiques annual exhibition is held each year from mid October for three weeks. Catalogues for this event are available by post.

When Ian Pout first came to Witney in 1977 as an antiques dealer little did he know that his shop, with the help of Gina Clayton and Janice Parr, would become the world famous **Teddy Bears of Witney**. Some eight years after opening near the centre of the town, the shop, with teddy bear collecting still in its infancy, was the first to specialise in selling new and old teddy bears and, today, the story continues. Now it is packed with over a thousand bears, each carefully selected from the world's best manufacturers and artists. The teddies are beautifully displayed amidst the antique furniture and other collectibles making for a

Teddy Bears of Witney, 99 High Street, Witney, Oxon OX8 6LY
Tel: 01993 702616

truly charming atmosphere. From the traditional Steiff and Merrythought bears through to contemporary bears designed by artists from all over the world, there is such a variety that everyone is sure to find a favourite.

However, this is no ordinary teddy bear shop. Ian is a keen collector himself and, on display in the shop, are two of the world's most famous bears: Aloysius and Alfonzo. Anyone who saw the television adaptation of Evelyn Waugh's *Brideshead Revisited* will remember Aloysius, the much loved bear belonging to Sebastian Flyte. Ian was able to purchase the bear used in the series, for a record price, and many will be surprised to learn that, for some 60 years, the bear sat in a Maine delicatessen. Named Deli, an exclusive limited edition of the bear has been made for Teddy Bears of Witney. Similarly, the famous manufacturer, Steiff, have produced a limited edition of Alfonzo, the red mohair bear that was given to Princess Xenia by her father the Grand Duke George of Russia in 1908. Dressed in a traditional Cossack tunic and trousers, the bear, following his owner's death in the USA in 1965, became the property of her daughter before being auctioned at Christies, London. For all teddy bear lovers, and children who never quite grew up, a trip to Teddy Bears of Witney is a must.

Situated down its own private driveway and within sight of the River Windrush, the aptly named **Windrush House** is the delightful home of Mr and Mrs Curtis. This charming couple moved here in 1997 and since than they have been offering superb bed and breakfast accommodation in a choice of two comfortable and well furnished guest rooms, each with private bathroom, television,

Windrush House, 55 Crawley Road, Witney, Oxon OX8 5HX
Tel: 01993 774454 Fax: 01993 709877 email: heraldic@compuserve.com

and tea and coffee making facilities. A contemporary style house, constructed in the mid 1970s by a builder as his private home, Windrush House is built on several levels which give it a unique atmosphere and the rooms are decorated with artefacts that Mr and Mrs Curtis have collected from their travels around the world. There are panoramic views over the superb lawned gardens down to the river and the house also has an integral heated swimming pool, along with a sauna, that is available for guests to use. Finally, a delicious breakfast, with vegetarian options, is served every morning and this adds the finishing touch to this wonderful bed and breakfast establishment.

AROUND WITNEY

CASSINGTON   MAP 1 REF C5
5 miles E of Witney off the A40

To the east of Witney lies the village of Cassington, with its fine Norman church, where the River Evenlode joins with the River Thames as it makes its way to Oxford.

Found on the banks of the River Evenlode and surrounded by some of the most beautiful and historic countryside that Oxfordshire has to offer, **Cassington Mill Caravan Park** is the ideal holiday location. Very much a family business, today the caravan park is managed by Margaret Partridge but it was established by her parents in the 1960s. Exceptionally well laid out and maintained, there are 83 excellent pitches for touring caravans, campers, and tents as well as a number of owner occupied static sites. The mature grounds of the site, which have been planted with a large variety of trees and shrubs, ensure that everyone has privacy as well as a charming and idyllic spot for their holiday. In deed, many of the sites overlook the calm and still waters of the River Evenlode.

As well as the delightful location and outlook, Cassington Mill Caravan Park has much to offer the family looking for a carefree holiday site. All the normal facilities that campers expect from a modern site are here including a well stocked site shop and the children are well catered for with the safe and well constructed playarea. Tucked away from main roads and with fishing permits available on the site, there is plenty here for everyone as well as the many attractions that this fascinating area has to offer being close to hand.

Cassington Mill Caravan Park, Eynsham Rd, Cassington, Witney, Oxon OX8 1DB
Tel: 01865 881081 Fax: 01865 884167

EYNSHAM
5 miles E of Witney on the A40

Map 1 ref C6

This ancient market town probably began as a Roman settlement and it was first referred to as a town in documents dating from as early as AD 571 when the name was spelt *Egonesham*. The site of an important Benedictine Abbey, founded in 1005, the town's early markets were controlled by the religious house. The town prospered and expanded in the early Middle Ages and, after the Black Death, a grant allowing two weekly markets was made in 1440.

Elements of the town's original medieval plan can still be seen, particularly around the market place, where there are some fine 16th- and 17th-century buildings that were constructed using materials from the abbey which was dismantled at the time of the Dissolution.

Found in the narrow streets of central Eynsham, **The Jolly Sportsman** is a wonderful ancient town pub parts of which were incorporated in a 15th-century monastery. Today, though, as the name suggests this is very much a sporting pub and, as well as having three football teams, one of which is 101 years old, there are darts, pool, and Aunt Sally teams in all the local leagues. Though taking part in such games is an important part of life here, the regulars are also keen horse racing fans and the giant television screen is an added bonus to armchair fans.

The Jolly Sportsman, 2 Lombard Street, Eynsham, Oxon OX8 1HT
Tel: 01865 881427

Traditionally decorated and comfortably furnished inside, the pub is the ideal place to come to for a delicious pint or two of beer and owners, Ruth Herring and Paul Clifton, ensure that this popular local's pub is also a welcoming place for people new to the area. Along with the drink, there is a traditional menu of unpretentious value for money pub food that ranges from sandwiches to Sunday roasts, that goes down a treat with all who visit here.

For a true home from home, look no further than **Parkview Guest House** in a quiet part of Eynsham. This traditional, detached large family house was built in the 1970s and, today, it is the home of June Foster and her husband. Modern in style and with lots of homely touches, such as the family photographs and oil paintings from Crete adorning the walls, this is certainly a house where guests can relax and take it easy. There are three comfortable and well equipped guest rooms, either with a separate or en-suite bathroom, and children are happily

Parkview Guest House, 49 Witney Road, Eynsham, near Witney, Oxon OX8 1PL Tel: 01865 880467

accommodated by arrangement. A full English or continental breakfast is served each morning and guests are also able to enjoy the delightful garden to the rear which, in the summer, is a real sun trap.

STANTON HARCOURT
4 miles SE of Witney off the B4449

MAP 1 REF C6

This beautiful village is noted for its historic manor house, **Stanton Harcourt Manor** which dates back to the 14th century. Famed for its well preserved medieval kitchen, one of the most complete to survive in this country, the house is also visited for its fine collection of antiques and the tranquil gardens. It was whilst staying here, from 1717 to 1718, that Alexander Pope translated Homer's great work, Iliad. Working in the 15th-century tower, a remainder of the original manor house, this is now referred to as **Pope's Tower**.

However, whilst the manor house draws people to the village, the splendid Norman **Church of St Michael** is also worthy of a visit. Naturally the Harcourt chapel dominates but there are other features of interest, including an intricate 14th century shrine to St Edburg.

STANDLAKE
5 miles SE of Witney on the A415

MAP 1 REF C6

Just to the south is the 13th-century **Newbridge**, the second oldest bridge across the River Thames. Like Radcot, Newbridge was the centre of a conflict during the

Civil War and the nearby pub, The Rose Revived, was used by Oliver Cromwell as a refreshment stopover during those years.

ASTON   MAP 1 REF B6
4 miles S of Witney on the B4449

Though the village green is known as The Square, it is, in fact, triangular and it lies at the heart of Aston. The Church of St John, built in 1839, has no distinguishing features, but does, unusually, have eight bells.

For a modern approach and style to fine English pottery, **Ellis Baughan Design** is the ideal place to visit. Started in the late 1980s by ceramic designer Jane Baughan, with the help of her husband Stephen, this now thriving cottage industry has grown and the company now supplies over 200 shops throughout Britain, Europe, and America. As the business has expanded, Stephen and Jane have gradually renovated the various farm buildings, all dating from the 1830s, to use as workshops finally culminating in the conversion of the milking and carving shed into an award winning showroom.

The distinctive pottery is made using traditional techniques and it is then hand painted using a specialised stencilling technique that gives the designs a fresh and crisp outline. The modern glazing and firing methods employed to finish the pieces ensures that the pottery is able to retain its vibrant colours despite the hard wear it will receive at the hands of dishwashers and microwaves. The light and airy shop displays the designs to maximum effect and with

Ellis Baughan Design, Kingsway Farm, Aston, near Bampton,
Oxon OX18 2BT Tel: 01993 852031 Fax: 01993 851877

over 40 different shapes and numerous designs, from the traditional patterns of English garden flowers and birds, to the more exotic African animals, there is sure to be a tea set or dinner service to suite every taste. Open seven days a week, the large showroom also incorporates a coffee shop where, naturally, the delicious home-made cakes and other tasty snacks are served on Ellis Baughan pottery. In April of 1999, they have just opened a new visitor and education centre, where people can have a guided tour to see teapots, plates, and jugs being made, with the addition of having a go at painting their own just to take home. For a unique insight into the traditional pottery industry, this superb pottery is well worth a visit. The shop and tea rooms are open seven days a week from 09.00 to 17.00 and Sundays 10.00 to 16.30. The pottery tours run from 1st April to 31st October, Monday to Friday 10.30 to 17.00.

BAMPTON
Map 1 ref B6

4½ miles SW of Witney on the B4449

Now a lovely old place, this ancient market town stood, until the mid-19th century, in the centre of an area of common land, and hence its full name - Bampton in the Bush. Edward the Confessor gave the estate of Bampton to his great friend and tutor, Leofric who, as one of the Royal Masons, was required to provide for the King when he visited. At the time of the Norman Conquest, a few years later, this was one of the largest settlements in Oxfordshire and as well as the important salt works, there was an early market. Prospering in the early Middle Ages on the back of the wool trade, a second market and an annual fair were granted in 1225.

Found in a cathedral-like close, the parish **Church of St Mary** is one of the largest in the county and the oldest parts of the building date back to Saxon times. However, what is seen today is chiefly the work of remodelling carried out in 1270 when both the spire and the aisle were built.

Perhaps, though, Bampton is best known for its Morris Dancers who, each Whit Monday, dance through the town carrying a sword on which is impaled a cake. Anyone offered a piece of the cake is considered to be in for good fortune.

RADCOT
Map 1 ref B7

7 miles SW of Witney on the A4095

This tiny hamlet boasts the oldest bridge across the River Thames. Built in 1154, **Radcot Bridge** represents an important crossing place and, as such, the hamlet has seen much conflict over the centuries. To the north of the bridge are the remains of a castle where, in 1141, King Stephen battled with the disenthroned Queen Matilda whilst, in the 13th century, King John fought his Barons before finally conceding and signing the Magna Carta.

Radcot Bridge

KELMSCOTT
9 miles SW of Witney off the A4095

MAP 1 REF A7

Found near the River Thames and dating from about 1570, **Kelmscott Manor House** was famously William Morris' country home from 1871 to 1896. Morris loved the house dearly and it is the scene of the end of his utopian novel *News from Nowhere*, in which he writes of a world where work has become a sought after pleasure.

Kelmscott Manor House

The house, which is open to visitors during the summer, has examples of Morris's work and memorabilia of Dante Gabriel Rosetti, who also stayed there. Rosetti is reputed to have found the village boring, so presumably the fact that he was in love with Morris' wife, Jane, drew him here. Morris himself is buried in the Churchyard, under a tombstone designed by his associate Philip Webb.

The church itself is interesting, the oldest parts dating from the late 12th century, and the village includes some fine farmhouses from around the end of the 17th and beginning of the 18th centuries.

FILKINS
MAP 1 REF A6

8 miles SW of Witney off the A361

This tiny Cotswold village is now the home of a flourishing community of craft workers and artists, many of whom work in restored 18th-century barns. Wool has played a great part in the wealth of this area and, also found in a converted barn is the **Cotswold Woollen Weavers**, a working weaving museum with an exhibition gallery and a mill shop.

Also found in this attractive village is the **Swinford Museum**, which concentrates on 19th-century domestic and rural trade and craft tools.

BRADWELL GROVE
MAP 1 REF A6

7 miles W of Witney off the A361

The 120 acres of park and garden which make up **The Cotswold Wild Life Park** are home to a whole host of animals, many of whom roam free in the wooded estate. Rhinos, zebras, ostriches, and tigers are just some of the animals in the spacious enclosures whilst tropical birds, monkeys, reptiles, and butterflies are all given the chance to enjoy the warmth of their natural habitat by staying indoors. With an adventure playground and a narrow-gauge railway, the park has something to offer every member of the family.

CARTERTON
MAP 1 REF B6

5 miles W of Witney on the B4020

One of the county's newest towns, Carterton began life as a settlement of small holdings before World War I and grew rapidly as a result of the establishment of RAF Brize Norton close by. It is now a lively and bustling town with all modern shopping facilities.

Found in the heart of this thriving market town, **The Beehive** is everything a busy centrally located pub should be - friendly and inviting. Managed by Sally and Steve Patterson, the pub is not only popular with the people of Carterton but also with those visiting the sights in the area. Solidly built in the 1930s, and with plenty of car parking to both the front and rear, there is ample space within for everyone to enjoy their time here in comfort. The lounge bar area runs the full

The Beehive, Black Bourton Road, Carterton, Oxon OX18 3HA
Tel: 01993 840813

length of the building, front to back, and in the quiet surroundings customers can relax with a drink and take in the display of old black and white photographs of the old town. The second bar is an altogether livelier place, with both pool and darts being played here as well as armchair sportsmen and women following their teams of the large TV screen. Decorated with a mass of cricket and tennis memorabilia there is no doubt that sports are taken seriously at the pub.

Open all day every day and with a late licence until 01.00 on Thursday, Friday, and Saturday evenings, this is certainly the place to come to for excellent food and drink and a good night out. Whilst Steve is acting as host behind the bar serving a good selection of real ales, Sally manages the catering. Covering all the traditional bar meals and snacks, including a delicious Sunday lunch, the delicious home-cooked meals here are well worth trying. A lively and friendly pub, customers can, during the summer months, also take advantage of the attractive beer garden.

6 In and Around Oxford

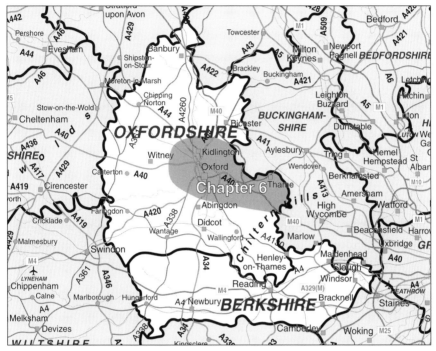

The county town of Oxfordshire, and the only place of any size, Oxford has dominated the surrounding area for centuries. The city of "dreaming spires", it was the influx of students and scholars in the 12th century which saw this walled Saxon town develop into the magnificent place it is today. With over 40 colleges making up the University, the oldest of which date from the 13th century, this seat of learning has influenced thinking all over the world for centuries. Home to some of the finest buildings in the country, the city deserves exploration and there is a wealth of beauty and interest to be discovered. However, it is not just a university city and, to the south, lies an industrial belt that is founded around William Morris's car factory at Cowley. Many of the rural villages around the city have been the homes of the city's famous intellectuals and, in particular, there is Elsfield to the north where both John Buchan and RD Blackmore had homes. During the 1920s at Garsington Manor, the socialite Lady Ottoline Morrell entertained the great artists, writers, and thinkers of the day including DH Lawrence, Bertrand Russell, and Aldous Huxley.

Other places in the area have a more notorious reputation: Cumnor Place where the suspected murder of Amy Dudley, instigated by her husband, Elizabeth I's lover, is said to have taken place; and Godstow Nunnery where not only did Henry II's mistress live and bear his children but where the nuns were said to prostitute themselves to Oxford's students.

OXFORD

The skyline of this wonderful city can be seen from many of the hilltops which surround it and the view is best described by the 19th-century poet, Matthew Arnold: "that sweet City with her dreaming spires." However, Oxford is not all beautiful, ancient buildings but a town of commerce and industry and, around the academic centre, there are suburbs and factories. A city which has been the centre of the country's intellectual, political, and architectural life for over 800 years, it is still an academic stronghold amidst fine architecture.

A walled town in Saxon times, which grew on a ford where the River Thames meets the River Cherwell, the first students came here in the 12th century when they were forced out of Europe's leading academic centre, Paris. Intellectual pursuits, then, were chiefly religious, and the town already had an Augustinian Abbey and, in a short space of time, Oxford became the country's seat of theological thinking. However, there was much tension between the townsfolk and the intellectuals and, in the 14th century, in a bid to protect their students, the university began to build colleges - enclosed quadrangles with large, sturdy front doors. The first colleges, Merton, Balliol, and University, where soon joined by others which still maintain their own individual style whilst also coming under the administration of the university.

Merton College was founded in 1264 by Walter de Merton, Lord Chancellor of England, as a small community of scholars from the income of his Surrey estates. Though the present buildings mostly date from the 15th to 17th centuries, Mob Quad is the university's oldest. The key feature of the college is its

Part of Oxford's Famous Skyline

splendid medieval library where the ancient books are still chained to the desks. Once considered the poor relation to other, wealthier colleges, **Balliol College** was founded in 1263 as an act of penance by John Balliol and for many years it was reserved for only the poor students. Most of the college buildings now date from the 19th century when the college was instrumental in spearheading a move towards higher academic standards. Thought by some to have been founded by Alfred the Great, **University College** was endowed in 1249 although the present college buildings are mostly 17th century. The poet Shelley was the college's most famous scholar though he was expelled in 1811 for writing a pamphlet on atheism. Whilst in Italy, at the age of 30, Shelley drowned and his memorial can be seen in the Front Quad.

One of the most beautiful colleges in the city, **Christ Church College**, was founded in 1525 as Cardinal College by Thomas Wolsey and then refounded as Christ Church in 1546 by Henry VIII after Wolsey had fallen from royal favour. The main gateway into the college leads through the bottom of Tom Tower (designed by Christopher Wren and home of the Great Tom bell) and into Tom Quad, the largest of the city's quadrangles. From here there is access to the rest of the college and also to the college's chapel. The only college chapel in the world to be designated a cathedral, Christ Church Cathedral is also England's smallest: it was founded in 1546 on the remains of a 12th-century building.

Another splendid college well worth a visit is **Magdalen College**, pronounced *'Maudlin'*, which has the most extensive grounds that include a riverside walk, a deer park, three quadrangles, and a series of glorious well manicured lawns. Founded in 1458 by William Waynflete, Bishop of Winchester, the colleges 15th-century bell tower is one of the city's most famous landmarks. During the 17th century, the college was at the centre of a revolt against James II's pro-Catholic policies and, a century later, academic standards here had slipped so far that Edward Gibbon, author of *The Decline and Fall of the Roman Empire*, called his time here as "the most idle and unprofitable" of his whole life.

Up until the end of the 19th century, these and all the other colleges, each with their own character, charm, and history, had solely catered for men but, times were changing and several women's only colleges were established. To-day, most of the colleges are open to both men and women though St Hugh's remains the preserve of ladies. The wealth of people that have spent time study-ing at Oxford is staggering and the long list of famous scholars includes numerous British Prime Ministers (including Harold Macmillan, Asquith, and Margaret Thatcher), Edward VIII as Prince of Wales, King Olaf of Norway, TS Eliot, JRR Tolkein, Charles Dodgson, Oscar Wilde, Sir John Betjeman, and John Wesley.

As well as the college buildings, Oxford has many interesting and magnifi-cent places to explore. At the city's central crossroads, unusually named **Carfax** and probably derived from the Latin for four-forked, is a tower, **Carfax Tower**, which is all that remains of the 14th-century Church of St Martin. A climb to the top of the tower offers magnificent views across the city. One of the most interesting buildings, the **Radcliffe Camera**, was built between 1737 and 1749 to a design by James Gibb. England's earliest example of a round reading room (camera is a medieval word for room), this splendid building still serves this purpose for the **Bodleian Library**. Named after Sir Thomas Bodley, a diplomat and a fellow of Merton College, Sir Thomas refounded the University Library in 1602 on the site of an earlier building. With over 5 1/2 million books it is one of the world's greatest libraries and one of only six entitled to a copy of every book published in Great Britain. The collection of early printed books and manuscripts is second only to the British Library in London and, though members

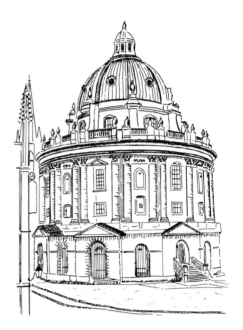

Radcliffe Camera

of the University can request to see any book here, this is not a lending library and they must be read and studied on the premises.

Close by is the **Clarendon Building**, the former home of the Oxford University Press and now part of the Bodleian. Designed by Nicholas Hawksmoor, a pupil of Christopher Wren, and constructed in the early 18th century, two of the original nine lead muses on the roof have had to be replaced by fibreglass replicas. Also in this part of the city is the **Bridge of Sighs**, part of Hertford College and a 19th-century copy of the original bridge which can be found in Venice. Here the bridge crosses a street rather than a canal.

However, Oxford's most famous building is the magnificent **Sheldonian Theatre** which was designed and built in the style of a Roman theatre by Christopher Wren between 1664 and 1668 whilst he was Professor of Astronomy at the University. It is still used today for its intended purpose, as a place for University occasions including metriculation, degree ceremonies, and the annual Encaenia, when honorary degrees are conferred on distinguished people. As well as the superb wooden interior, the ceiling has 32 canvas panels, depicting Truth descending on the Arts, which are the work of Robert Streeter, court painter to Charles II.

Naturally, the city has several museums and the best place to start is at the innovative **Oxford Story**, which presents a lively review of the last 800 years of university life, from the Middle Ages to the present day. The **Museum of Ox-**

Bridge of Sighs, Hertford College

ford, with a different style, also covers the story of Oxford through a series of permanent displays showing various archaeological finds.

First opened in 1683 and the oldest museum in the country, the **Ashmolean Museum** was originally established to house the collection of the John Tradescants, father and son. On display in this internationally renowned museum are archaeological collections from Britain, Europe, Egypt, and the Middle East; Italian, Dutch, Flemish, French, and English old masters; far eastern art, ceramics, and lacquer work; and Chinese bronzes. Found in the Ashmolean's original building and built up this century is the **Museum of the History of Science**, a remarkable collection of early scientific instruments including Einstein's blackboard and a large silver microscope made for George III.

Found in a splendid high Victorian building, near the University Science Area, is the **University Museum** where the remains of a dodo, extinct since around 1680, and a mass of fossilised dinosaur remains are on display. Also here is the **Pitt Rivers Museum**, with its interesting collection taken from all over the world.

Musicians will enjoy the **Bate Collection of Historical Instruments**, whilst those captivated by old masters should take time to visit the **Christ Church Picture Gallery**, with its collection of works by Tintoretto, Van Dyck, Leonardo da Vinci, and Michaelangelo.

Another place worthy of a visit and a particularly peaceful haven in the city are the **Botanic Gardens**, down by the river. Founded in 1621, when plants were the only source of medicines, this was a teaching garden where the plants grown here were studied for their medicinal and scientific use. The rose garden here commemorates the work of Oxford's scientists in the discovery and use of penicillin.

Oxford is also the place where the River Thames changes its name to the poetic Isis and, at **Folly Bridge**, not only are there punts for hire but river trips can be taken, both up and down stream, throughout the day and evening.

Found right in the heart of this bustling city, yet in an oasis of calm, **Edgars Restaurant** is reached through the archway in Carfax Tower. Once used as a graveyard this charming courtyard and gardens is the perfect place for sophisticated dining and Edgars provides just that either inside or al fresco if the weather permits. Open through out the day and catering for all ages, this busy cosmopolitan restaurant was

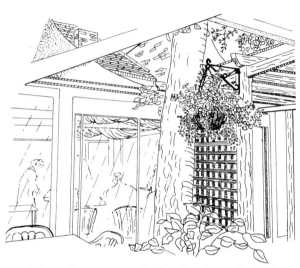

Edgars Restaurant, Carfax Gardens, Oxford, Oxon OX1 1EP Tel: 01865 790622

started in 1996 by Leigh-Anne El-Barhdadi and her own experiences of travelling the world are reflected in the delicious range of dishes and snacks available. From breakfast through into the evening, the menu provides customers with a tantalising choice of tasty and exotic dishes that are sure to make this one of the most popular place in the city.

Close to the centre of Oxford, yet in a residential area and with good restaurants near by, **Lonsdale Guest House** is a large turn of the century Victorian townhouse that is owned and personally run by Christine and Roland Adams. The couple have been here since 1967 and, over the years, they

Lonsdale Guest House, 312 Banbury Rd, Oxford, Oxon OX2 7ED Tel & Fax: 01865 554872

have grown the guest house business into the marvellous establishment it is today. Ideally suited to both business visitors and those visiting Oxford, this spacious house has eight comfortable and well appointed guest rooms, most of which have en-suite facilities. Holders of the Heart Beat Award for Healthy Eating, there is a full range of dishes, traditional, vegetarian, and continental, for breakfast and the couple also have an unusual gadget for topping boiled eggs that is sure to raise a smile. A pleasant and relaxing place to stay, Lonsdale Guest House has parking either at the front of the building or on a side road.

Located just over a mile from the city centre, **Green Gables** is an attractive Edwardian town house that was built in 1914 for a local Oxford merchant. Well cared for and maintained over the years, this spacious house retains much of its

original atmosphere and comfort. Owned and personally run as an excellent guest house by Narinder and Parvesh Bhella, this characterful detached property offers guests a choice of nine well appointed guest rooms. Two of the rooms are on the ground floor, one having been fully equipped with wheelchair users in mind, and there is a ramp to the front door and no internal steps. All the rooms are spacious and bright and, as the house is also screened from the road by mature trees, guests are sure of a comfortable and relaxing night's sleep. A superb place

Green Gables, 326 Abingdon Road,
Oxford, Oxon OX1 4TE
Tel: 01865 725870 Fax: 01865 723115
email: green.gables@virgin.net

to stay, where all guests' needs are well catered for, a substantial breakfast is served each morning. Both Narinder and Parvesh know Oxford well and can advise guests on places to eat out, exciting night life, places to visit, and things to do.

AROUND OXFORD

ELSFIELD   MAP 1 REF D6
2 miles N of Oxford off the A40

The village was the home of the author, John Buchan, from 1919 to 1935, when he left to fill his appointment as Governor General of Canada. During his time at Elsfield Manor House he wrote several of books including *Midwinter*, published in 1923, which begins on nearby Otmoor. Buchan's grave can be seen in the churchyard of St Thomas' Church, the oldest parts of which date from the 12th century. RD Blackmore, author of *Lorna Doone*, also lived here as a child whilst his father was the vicar. One of his books, *Cripps the Carrier*, published in 1876, was set in the surrounding area and Cripps' cottage is said to have stood on the road to the nearby village of Beckley.

ISLIP   MAP 1 REF D5
6 miles N of Oxford on the B4027

Although most of Oxfordshire is a region of rich farmland, to the east of the village lies **Otmoor**, a desolate area of peat-covered bogland. However, the land has been jealously guarded by the local people over the years: attempts to enclose and drain the land in the early 19th century was met by great resistance which led to several arrests and, more recently, attempts to route the M40 across the moor were successfully opposed.

MERTON   MAP 1 REF E5
7 miles N of Oxford off the A41

To the west of the 14th-century village church lies a thatched Tithe Barn which probably dates from the 15th century. There are also some attractive old houses to be found in the village.

NOKE   MAP 1 REF D5
4 miles N of Oxford off the B4027

Another village on the edge of Otmoor, Noke was reputedly lost by the Duchess of Marlborough during a game of cards in the late 19th century. Inside the village **Church of St Giles** can be seen a quite gruesome carving from the 17th century.

STANTON ST JOHN   MAP 1 REF E6
3½ miles NE of Oxford off the B4027

The village is named after John de St John, a 12th-century Lord of the Manor of Stanton, and it has ancient connections with New College, Oxford, which still owns several buildings here. It is an attractive place with sturdy stone houses and farms grouped around the 12th-century Church of St John. Opposite the church, lies the house of John White, a farmer's son, who became a Fellow of New College and went on to be one of the founders of Massachusetts, America.

FOREST HILL
3 miles E of Oxford on the B4027

MAP 1 REF E6

In 1642, the poet John Milton was married to a local girl at the pretty village church. However, the couple (he was 31 and she was only 17) parted company after only a short time and soon afterwards Milton wrote the first of his controversial pamphlets on divorce.

WHEATLEY
4 miles E of Oxford on the A40

MAP 1 REF E6

This former quarry village still retains several old buildings of which the most interesting is a curious, conical **Lock-up**.

To the west, close to the M40, are the famous **Waterperry Gardens** of Waterperry House. Laid out around the Georgian house, which unlike the gardens is not open to the public, there is the additional attraction of a Saxon church, complete with wooden-hatted belfry, to be seen. Established as a residential gardening school for women in the 1930s, Waterperry is now owned by the School of Economic Science and it is part pleasure garden and part working nursery. Set in 83 acres of Oxfordshire countryside, there are magnificent herbaceous, shrub, and heather borders, alpine gardens, rock gardens and a newly laid out formal garden. The nurseries and greenhouses are a treasure house for keen gardeners. The gardens are host each summer to Art in Action, bringing together many of the world's finest craftsmen.

TIDDINGTON
7 miles E of Oxford on the A418

MAP 2 REF E6

Just to the west of the village lies **Rycote Chapel**, a private chapel that is found amongst the trees. Built in 1449 and still with some of its original seating, the real treat here is are the glorious 17th-century fittings which include two magnificent domes and canopies pews. One may have been used by Elizabeth I, who is known to have stayed at the long since vanished mansion here, whilst the other was installed for Charles I.

Found on the main road through the village, **The Fox** is a charming old coaching inn that has lost none of its character over the years. Still on a major route, the pub continues to offer travellers excellent food and drink whilst they take a break in their journey. The inn too is also a central point of the village and, as well as providing a local meeting place, there are several teams based here including darts and the local game of Aunt Sally. Managed by Martin

The Fox, Oxford Road, Tiddington, Oxon OX9 2LH
Tel: 01844 339245 Fax: 01844 338556

Blackburn and Gavin Smith since 1998, these two well travelled friends have created a warm and friendly pub that is an ideal place to bring the whole family. The interior reflects the age of the building and the olde worlde feel is enhanced by the mass of gleaming brass and copper ware that is on display throughout. As well as serving an excellent pint of real ale, there is always a choice of four, The Fox has an enviable reputation for the delicious meals that are prepared here under Gavin's watchful eye. Not only do the menus include many favourites there are also some interesting and unusual dishes that must have been influenced by the friends' trips abroad. Finally, for warm summer days there are beer gardens to the front and rear of the pub, ideal for enjoying the sunshine as well as the hospitality, and the pub has ample car parking.

THAME   MAP 2 REF F6
11 miles E of Oxford on the A418

Founded in 635 as an administrative centre for the Bishop of Dorchester, Thame first became a market town in the 13th century and its importance as a commercial centre is evident by the wide main street it still has today. Lined with old inns and houses, some of which go back to the 15th century, this is a delightful place to visit.

The imposing **Church of St Mary**, tucked away at one end of the High Street, was built in the 13th century though the aisles were widened in the 14th century and the tower was heightened in the 15th century. In the centre of the chancel is a monument to Lord John Williams, and his wife, who was notorious for having helped burn Archbishop Thomas Cranmer in the 16th century.

To the west of the church lies the **Prebendal House** which, in its oldest parts, dates from the 13th century. A prebend was an income granted to a priest by a Cathedral or Collegiate Church and, at Thame, the prebend was established in around 1140 by Lincoln Cathedral. A special residence for the holders of the office was first mentioned in 1234.

The town also has a famous **Grammar School**, housed in a Tudor building in Church Lane. The schoolmaster's house faces the road and over the doorway are the arms of Lord Williams, who founded the school in 1558. John Hampden, one of the Parliamentary leaders during the Civil War, was at school here and he also died at Thame. An MP from 1621, Hampden sat in Parliament whenever it had not been dissolved by the King. He denied the right of the King to raise taxes without the sanction of Parliament and in 1636 refused to pay the 'ship tax' the King was demanding. As a result he was successfully prosecuted and, at the same time, became a popular leader in the country. When the Civil War broke out he raised a regiment of infantry for the Parliamentary Army and fought with great bravery at Edgehill and Reading. However, he was wounded at the battle of Chalgrove Field in June 1643 and was carried back to Thame, where he died some days later in an inn which stood on the High Street.

A little to the south of the town is **Thame Park**, a house built on the site of a Cistercian Abbey founded in 1138 and which, after the Dissolution, became the home of Lord Williams. The present, privately owned house incorporates some of the former monastic buildings to which has been added a gracious Georgian house.

This is also a town with an amazing number of inns and public houses. Whilst the oldest is the 15th-century Birdcage Inn, the most fascinating and well known is **The Spread Eagle**. A favourite place with the local farmers, in 1922 the inn was taken over by John Fothergill. He made little attempt to befriend the farmers and continued running the inn in the traditional manner. After several attempts to build up trade one way or another were very successful, he almost deliberately began to discourage most of the clientele he had. Gradually a new kind of customer began to replace the old. Fothergill's many society friends passed the word around and people came up from London to savour the delights of The Spread Eagle. Word soon reached the ears of the Dons and wealthy undergraduates of Oxford.

However, John Fothergill did not entirely approve of this sector of society and this led to him making an unfortunate mistake. One day he received a letter from Queen's College, Oxford requesting that he prepare a special dinner for two. Assuming that the letter had been sent by a rich undergraduate and, always keen to teach people a lesson, he replaced their oysters with winkles, substituted chicken for pheasant, and stuffed cucumbers instead of aubergines. When the diners arrived they turned out to be the most eminent gourmets in the entire university, TW Allen, a Fellow of Queens College, and Dr Cowley, the Curator of the Bodleian. One consolation was that Fothergill was able to serve them with the best wines! John Fothergill sold The Spread Eagle in 1931 after having lost a sizeable amount of money. Today it is still one of the most superb places in this area and well worth a visit.

Situated in the centre of the town is the striking **Munch 'n' Judy**, a charming tea room that is owned and personally run by Alison Phillips. The single-fronted, black and white, 16th-century shop opens into a delightful, intimate room, with a lovely olde worlde fireplace and then into a similar room to the rear. Warm and cosy, both of the café's rooms have a mass of pictures hanging from the walls and knick-knacks lying around which give the place a truly homely feel. Open every day except Mondays, Munch 'n' Judy is a popular place with the people of Thame and particularly with those who enjoy a traditional English tea room. Alison does all the cooking herself and, whilst admitting to being a highly strung chef, she has a warm personality and great sense of humour that is sure to endear her to all customers. As well as the menu, which covers everything from breakfast to afternoon tea, there is always a mouthwatering list of daily specials that, as with everything else, are prepared by Alison. Certainly a place not to be missed, Munch 'n' Judy is well worth seeking out.

Munch 'n' Judy, 57 North Street, Thame, Oxon OX9 3BH Tel: 01844 213007

TETSWORTH
MAP 2 REF F6
10 miles E of Oxford on the A40

Just to the southwest of Thame, at Tetsworth, can be found **The Swan at Tetsworth**, which is set in a magnificent Grade II listed building dating back some 500 years. Following an extensive renovation programme, The Swan opened in January 1995 offering an excellent choice of quality antiques plus a superb gourmet restaurant. Browsing through this fascinating building visitors will find hidden treasures in over 40 rooms of antiques. Each room has its own special charm with fine antiques ranging from a silver spoon for a few pounds to exquisite Georgian furniture. There is something for everyone with furniture, pictures, prints, books, silver, ceramics, sporting goods, textiles, rugs, lighting, and many more items to catch the eye of the discerning buyer. There

The Swan at Tetsworth, High Street, Tetsworth, near Thame,
Oxon OX9 7AB Tel: 01844 281777 Fax: 01844 281770

is also a Garden Statuary Area nestled within the grounds of The Swan where customers can wander through a maze of garden furniture, urns, chimney pots, and many other outdoor antiquities. The Antiques Centre is open seven days a week from 10.00 am to 6.00 pm (including Bank Holidays) and visitors are invited to browse at their leisure where there is always excellent advice on hand to help visitors gain the most out of their antique furniture.

The Swan Restaurant has an enviable reputation for the modern, country character of the cuisine served in the delightful setting of the restaurant. The interesting menu offers a sophisticated blend of traditional flavours with tastes from around the world. In addition to the lunch and dinner à la carte and table d'hôte menu (weekdays only) the restaurant hosts a programme of speciality evenings where a themed menu is designed to intrigue the palate of the diner and provide the opportunity to flaunt the skills of The Swan's top chef. Reservations are recommended.

GREAT HASELEY

MAP 2 REF E6

7 miles SE of Oxford off the A329

This large village is home to some fine stone houses, some old thatched cottages, and its original stone windmill. The village church too is pleasant, with its high Norman boor, 13th-century chancel, and numerous monuments. One of the past vicars here was the father of the architect, Sir Christopher Wren, also called Christopher.

Situated in the heart of this attractive and picturesque village, **The Plough** is a mainly thatched typical country pub that dates from the 16th century. Owned and personally run by Pauline and Charles, well known members of the village community, this is a very popular place that is well frequented by locals as well as visitors to the area. As charming and quaint inside as the exterior would suggest, there are low ceilings, exposed beams, a stone flagged floor, and the building's original bread oven can still be seen. The bar area is cosy and comfortable and is not only the place for a quiet drink and a chance to catch up on the local news, but also the place for playing many of the traditional pub games including cribbage, darts, and Aunt Sally. The Plough is also well known for its delicious menu of tasty dishes and bar snacks. With a very popular lunchtime trade, as well as the usual menu, Friday is the day for fresh fish and this is where the pub excels. With ample parking and an attractive and colourful beer garden, The Plough is a place well worth seeking out.

The Plough, Rectory Road, Great Haseley, Oxon OX44 7JQ
Tel: 01844 279283

GREAT MILTON
MAP 1 REF E6
6½ miles SE of Oxford off the A329

As well as being home to the splendid Georgian **Great House**, the village also has a 13th-century church that is full of interesting and unusual features, including a display cabinet containing the instruments used by the church's orchestra before the organ was installed. Beside the church, in a 15th-century building is the famous restaurant of chef Raymond Blanc, **Le Manoir aux Quat' Saisons**.

MILTON COMMON
MAP 2 REF E6
7½ miles SE of Oxford off the A329

Though Sylvia and David Mott have lived in their attractive bungalow, **Byways Guest House**, since the late 1970s, this charming couple only started the bed and breakfast business recently. Surrounded by a large well tended and mature garden, complete with a pond, this superb detached home has been stylishly furnished and decorated with a mix of modern and antique styles. The two attractive and comfortable guest rooms are of the same high standard and are

Byways Guest House, Old London Road, Milton Common, Thame, Oxon OX9 2JR Tel: 01844 279386

both totally colour coordinated with great attention to detail. After a relaxing and peaceful night's sleep, guests are then treated to a magnificent home-cooked breakfast which incorporates many organic foods including homemade breads, preserves, and Sylvia also bakes a scrumptious cherry cake.

  The Three Pigeons is situated on the old main road between Oxford and London and it was built in 1682 as a coaching inn to serve this once busy stretch of road. However, not all the inn's customers were travellers as, in years gone by, public hangings took place just outside the inn and records suggest

The Three Pigeons, Milton Common, Oxon OX9 2JN
Tel: 01844 279247

that over 2000 spectators would turn up to see the gruesome spectacle. Today, fortunately, though The Three Pigeons still serves travellers well, there are no such events in the area to draw the crowds. A delightful old building, with plenty of parking space, the inn, which is managed by licensees David and Olwyn Skinner, is just the place to stop for refreshment. AS well as serving a wide range of beers, ales, and lagers, The Three Pigeons has an excellent reputation for the high standard of its cuisine. David is a trained chef himself and has worked in many of the top restaurants and, with the help of another chef, the menu served here runs from traditional pub food right through to full à la carte. With two bar areas, a large dining area, and a large garden with seating, there is plenty of space for all to enjoy the delicious and imaginative meals served here. Finally, in the true tradition of a coaching inn, The Three Pigeons also has a number of double and single en-suite guest rooms, all of which are well furnished and decorated.

A stay at **Lower Chilworth Farm** is a must for garden lovers, those who enjoy the countryside, and people seeking a retreat from the madding crowds. Occupied by Miriam and Michael Hedges, who have been here since the early 1970s, the large family farmhouse stands amid the most glorious garden which Miriam has created over the years they have been here. The garden is part formal and part informal and contains a vast number of different species of plants, shrubs, and trees. As well as the lake, visitors can wander along the pathways, beneath arches, and admire the labours of Miriam's all consuming hobby. Michael, on the other hand, creates nature trails, which the house collie

Lower Chilworth Farm, Milton Common, Thame, Oxon OX9 2JS
Tel: 01844 279593

is happy to lead people round. From their spacious and stylish farmhouse, the couple offer charming bed and breakfast accommodation in a choice of three en-suite guest rooms. Naturally, there are views over the gardens to the farmland beyond and this really is the ideal place for a relaxing stay.

CUDDESDON   Map 1 ref E6

4½ miles SE off the A329

For over 400 years, this prosperous village was the home of the Bishops of Oxford although their grand house was first burnt down by Oliver Cromwell and then again, by accident, in 1960. Today, the village is dominated by **Ripon College**, a theological school that has trained generations of Anglican clergy. A large Victorian building with modern extensions, it is very much in contrast to the nearby All Saints' Church which, though mainly Victorian, is originally Norman.

GARSINGTON   Map 1 ref E6

4 miles SE of Oxford off the B480

The main reason for visiting this village, which is surprisingly rural considering it's so close to Oxford, is the 16th-century **Garsington Manor**. Between 1915 and 1927, this was the home of the socialite Lady Ottoline Morrell who, along with her husband Philip, were unflaggingly hospitable to a whole generation of writers, artists, and intellectuals including Katherine Mansfield, Lytton Strachey,

Clive Bell, Siegfried Sassoon, DH Lawrence, TS Eliot, Rupert Brooke, Bertrand Russell, and Aldous Huxley. Huxley based an account of a country house party in his novel *Crome Yellow* on his experiences at Garsington, thereby causing a rift with his hostess. She found his description all too apt, and felt betrayed. Huxley insisted that he had not meant any harm, but she remained hurt and they were estranged for some time.

It seems that Lady Ottoline was not very lucky in the artists on whom she lavished her attention and hospitality. DH Lawrence also quarrelled with her after drawing a less than flattering, but clearly recognisable, portrait of life at her house in *Women in Love*:

The house itself is attractive built from stone with mullioned windows and dormer windows under gables projecting from the attics.

Garsington's other claim to literary fame is that Rider Haggard was sent to the school run by the Rev HJ Graham at the rectory in 1866. The present house is later, built in 1872, but across the road from the Church is a 16th-century gateway from the rectory he would have known. While there Haggard became friendly with a local farmer named Quartermain whom he must have remembered with affection as he used the name for his hero, many years later, in his novel *King Solomon's Mines*.

The village **Church of St Mary** is a pleasant and cosy building with fine views to the south over the Chilterns from its hill top position, but it also looks over the industrial belt to the south of Oxford. Though the interior is chiefly Victorian, the church has retained its Norman tower and inside there is an elegant memorial to Lady Ottoline.

COWLEY   MAP 1 REF D6

2 miles SE of Oxford on the A4142

This suburb of Oxford is home to William Morris's motor car factory which was one of the first to produce cars on a production line system.

SANDFORD ON THAMES   MAP 1 REF D6

3 miles S of Oxford off the A4074

The large weir to the side of Sandford Lock on the River Thames, **Sandford Lasher**, is where the boy who inspired Peter Pan was drowned in May 1921. The boy, Michael Llewelyn Davies, an Oxford student, was a close family friend of Peter Pan's creator, JM Barrie.

SUNNINGWELL   MAP 1 REF D6

4 miles SW of Oxford off the A34

Roger Bacon, the medieval philosopher and scientist who invented the magnifying glass, is believed to have used the tower of the village **Church of St Leonard** as an observatory for his studies in astronomy after his return to Oxford from

Paris in about 1250. A Franciscan monk , Bacon's scholarship caused such problems due to the prejudices of his time that the head of the Franciscan Order had him imprisoned in 1277 for 'suspected novelties' - he was only released just before his death in 1292.

The church itself is an interesting one, with a unique seven-sided porch known as the Jewel Porch after John Jewel, who was rector at the time of its construction about 155l. There is also an extremely interesting east window designed by JP Seddon, who restored the church in 1877. Seddon was a friend of William Morris and the pre-Raphaelites and his window is clearly influenced by their aesthetic ideas.

CUMNOR
Map 1 ref C6
4 miles W of Oxford off the A420

In this village is the site of **Cumnor Place**, where, in September 1560, the body of Amy Dudley, the wife of Robert Dudley, Earl of Leicester and a favourite of Elizabeth I, was found at the foot of a staircase. The house belonged, at the time, to Anthony Forster and he is widely suspected of having arranged her death, at the behest of Robert Dudley, so that he would then be free to marry his lover, the Queen.

The village Church of St Michael, first founded in Saxon times, is also worth investigating. There is a statue of Elizabeth I (considered by some to have been party to the plot to do away with her favourite's wife), memorials to Amy, and the ornate tomb of Anthony Forster.

WOLVERCOTE
Map 1 ref D6
3½ miles NW of Oxford off the A34

The village is know to many who enjoy a quiet pub as this is the home of the famous **Trout Inn** which stands beside a branch of the River Thames and has been providing refreshment to scholars, dons, and tourists alike for many years. Built in 1737, not only was Charles Dodgson a frequent visitor but viewers of the *Inspector Morse* television series will recognise the building as it is also one of the policeman's favourite haunts.

Since the 17th century, the village has also been a major producer and supplier of paper used by the university press for their bibles. The present paper mill, which dates from the 1950s, is the only large building here and so cannot be missed.

All that remains of ruined **Godstow Nunnery**, found on the banks of the River Thames, are the walls of the garden and the shell of the chapel. Established in 1138, the nunnery was soon to gain a notorious reputation as Henry II made a mistress of one of the nuns, Rosamund Clifford, the daughter of local nobleman, Walter de Clifford. She bore the king several children and was the cause of much jealousy from his Queen, Eleanor of Aquitaine, who is alleged to have ordered Rosamund poisoned. She died in the nunnery's hospice, in 1176, and was buried here only to have her body removed from the grounds by the Bishop of Lincoln in 1191 as the ground was too sacred for such a woman. However, later her body was secretly returned to the nunnery. Godstow's notorious history does not end here as, later, the nuns became well known for prostituting themselves to the local Oxford scholars.

KIDLINGTON
Map 1 ref D5

5 miles NW of Oxford on the A4260

Situated between the Oxford Canal and the River Cherwell, until the 1930s, this was a small collection of farms, cottages, and Georgian houses but, after being designated a garden suburb, a mass of pre and post-war housing was built. However, the attractive 13th-century St Mary's Church survives, along with some other of the village's original buildings, and they are concentrated in the town centre. In 1840, the famous pharmacist, and ancestor of the conductor, Thomas Beecham came to the village and here he made his first pills by extracting the essence from grass near his uncle's cottage.

7 Northwest Oxfordshire

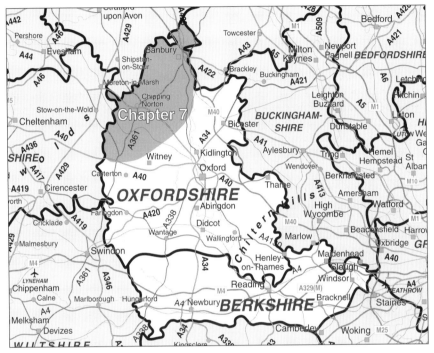

This northwestern region of the county lies almost wholly in the Cotswold area, a place of honey coloured stone buildings and quaint old market towns. Burford, the Gateway to the Cotswolds, and Chipping Norton are typical of the towns found further west, in Gloucestershire, and they both owe their early prosperity to the wool gleaned from the Cotswold sheep.

To the east lies Woodstock, an ancient place which was once home to a medieval royal palace that was used as a hunting lodge for trips into Wychwood Forest, the royal hunting ground which stood to the west of the town and extended as far as Burford. Today, the town, a wealth of antique and tea shops, is best known for the magnificent Blenheim Palace, the thank you from a grateful Queen Anne to her loyal subject the Duke of Marlborough. Built in the early 18th century to the designs of John Vanbrugh and set in the landscaped grounds of Capability Brown, this superb palace is now a World Heritage site. Though grand and opulent, it was also the birthplace of Winston Churchill and his modest room there is in contrast to the elaborately decorated and furnished reception rooms.

The vast Blenheim estate dominates the area around Woodstock and many of the villages have connections with the family and the house. One, in particular, is worthy of a visit: on a bleak November day in 1965, Sir Winston Churchill was laid to rest in a simple grave in Bladon church.

The River Evenlode divides this region into two and along this stretch the riverbanks are followed by the Oxfordshire Way. Some 65 miles long, this marked footpath passes through some of the most rural and scenic parts of the county from its start at Bourton-on-the-Water to its end at Henley-on-Thames.

WOODSTOCK

Situated in the Glyme Valley, in an area of land that was originally part of the Wychwood Forest, the name of this elegant Georgian market town means a *'place in the woods'*. To the north of the River Glyme is the old Saxon settlement whilst, on the opposite bank, lies the new town which was developed by Henry II in the 13th century to serve the Royal Park of Woodstock. There had been hunting lodges for the Kings of England here long before the Norman Invasion and it was Henry I who established the deer park around the manor of Woodstock.

It was whilst at his palace here that Henry II first seduced Rosamund, who he is said to have housed in a bower in the park. One story tells how Henry's wife, Queen Eleanor, managed to uncover the couple by following an unravelled ball of silk that had become attached to her husband's spur. Rosamund, the daughter

Woodstock

of a local nobleman, became a nun at the infamous Godstow Nunnery where she also bore him several children.

This long since disappeared medieval palace was also the birthplace of the Black Prince in 1330 and Princess Elizabeth was held prisoner here in 1558 during the reign of her sister, Queen Mary. On ascending the throne, a grateful Elizabeth I granted the town a second weekly market and two fairs for its loyalty. The palace was damaged during the Civil War, when it served as a Royalist garrison and the last remains were demolished in 1710.

Whilst the new town became an important coaching centre, many of the old inns survive to this day, and prospered as a result of the construction of the Oxford Canal and, later the railway, in 1886. The old town's trade was glovemaking and traditionally a pair of new gloves are presented to a visiting monarch. Today's visitors can look round both the factory and showroom of **Woodstock Gloves**.

The town is also home to the **Oxfordshire County Museum**, which is housed in the wonderful and imposing 16th-century **Fletcher's House**. As well as the permanent displays on the life of the county through the centuries, the museum has a peaceful garden open to the public and, at the entrance, can be seen the town's old stocks.

However, it is the magnificent **Blenheim Palace**, one of only four sites in the country to be included on the World Heritage List, which brings most people to Woodstock. The estate and cost of building the palace was a gift from a grateful Queen Anne to the heroic John Churchill, 1st Duke of Marlborough, for his victory at the Battle of Blenheim during the Spanish War of Succession. However, the Queen's gratitude ran out before the building work was complete and the duke had to pay the remainder of the costs himself.

As his architect, Marlborough chose Sir John Vanbrugh whose life was even more colourful than that of his patron. He was at the same time both an architect (although at the time of his commission he was relatively unknown) and a playwright, and he also had the distinction of having been imprisoned in the Bastille, Paris. The result of his work was the Italianate palace (built between 1705 and 1722), which is now seen sitting in a very English park that was later landscaped by Capability Brown. Unfortunately, once completed, the new house did not meet with universal approval: it was ridiculed by Jonathan Swift and Alexander Pope whilst Marlborough's wife, Sarah, who seems to have held the family purse strings, delayed paying Vanbrugh as long as possible.

A marvellous, grand place with a mass of splendid paintings, furniture, porcelain, and silver on show, visitors will also be interested in the more intimate memorabilia of Sir Winston Churchill. Born here in 1874, Churchill was a cousin of the 9th Duke and the family name remains Churchill.

First grown by George Kempster, a tailor from Old Woodstock, the Blenheim Orange apple took its name from the palace. Though the exact date of the first apple is unknown, Kempster himself died in 1773 and the original tree blew down in 1853. So famous did the spot where the tree stood become that it is said London-bound coaches and horses used to slow down so that passengers might gaze upon it.

One of the 'Potato Pubs' owned by Ian Leslie, **The Kings Head**, in the centre of this historic town, is an attractive old building dating from around 1700. A typical old local, but with a high standard of decoration and furnishing, this is a wonderful place to stop at for some excellent food, drink, and company. The traditional atmosphere found here is enhanced by the roaring log fire in winter, the old prints on the walls, and the mass of brass and copper ware that is found everywhere. In keeping with the common philosophy of the other pubs in the group, The Kings Head offers customers good value food and drink in comfortable surroundings and one glance at the menu will confirm that this is certainly achieved. As well as featuring a range of filled jacket potatoes, there are many favourites and, though this is a popular place for meals, the pub also plays hosts to several darts teams and has an Aunt Sally pitch.

The Kings Head, 11 Park Lane, Woodstock, Oxon OX20 1UD Tel: 01993 812164 Fax: 01993 811092

Harriet's, in the centre of Woodstock, is a delightful cake shop, patisserie, and tea rooms that is housed in a charming early 17th-century building that is named Ye Anciente House. Although much altered over the years, there are several original features still to be seen including the early 17th-century carved lintel with its Sun Alliance Fire insurance plaque in place and, also carved over the front, the initials WTE, which are probably those of Thomas Williams, mayor of Woodstock from 1630 to 1632. With its double fronted windows, stepping into this shop and tea rooms is like stepping back in time. The beams and

Harriet's, Ye Anciente House, High Street, Woodstock, Oxon OX20 1TF
Tel: 01993 811231

wooden floors add to the traditional atmosphere and the old fashioned shop counter displays the delicious and mouthwatering cakes and pastries that are all made locally. Those with time to linger can enjoy the relaxed air of the tea rooms as well as the same superb array of cakes and French style pastries and tarts. The tea rooms menu also includes a tasty range of hot and cold savoury snacks and light meals and a wonderful English breakfast that is served until noon. Open every day, throughout the year, this is an excellent place to stop and enjoy some excellent fayre.

AROUND WOODSTOCK

WOOTTON   MAP 3 REF C5
2 miles N of Woodstock on the B4027

A quiet and pleasant village, with a bridge over the River Glyme, the 13th-century **Church of St Mary** saw the wedding, in 1879, of the diarist, Francis Kilvert and Elizabeth Anne Rowland. Unfortunately, Kilvert died of peritonitis just over a month later.

Built in 1637 by Thomas Killingworth, the **Killingworth Castle Inn**, on the edge of the village of Wootton, once served as a coaching halt on the London to Worcester road. Run by the Killingworth family for several generations, this attractive and picturesque inn is now owned and managed by Maureen and Paul Barrow. Retaining much of its original character and charm, the interior of the Killingworth Castle is a cosy and comfortable mix of the building's original features, such as the beamed ceiling and large stone fireplaces, with more recent additions like the pine scrubtop tables in the bar and the small games room.

As one of the first pubs in the country to be awarded the new Cask Marque accreditation, a system to ensure the quality of real ales, visitors can be sure that all of the cask conditioned ales at the Killingworth Castle Inn will be in tip top condition. In addition, there is a selection of lagers, keg beers, and spirits, an important feature being a sizeable selection of malt whiskies. For those preferring wine the full list of reasonably priced quality wines is offered by the glass as well as by the bottle. An extensive menu of à la carte dishes, ranging from

**Killingworth Castle Inn, Glympton Road, Wootton, Woodstock,
Oxon OX20 1EJ Tel & Fax: 01993 811401 email: kil.cast@btinternet.com**

snacks to three course meals, is served every day, at lunch times and evenings.

Live music is an important feature at the Killingworth Castle. Folk music, every Friday evening, has been a continuous event for the past 20 years or so. More recently, Maureen and Paul have added live jazz, presenting national and international performers on the first and third Wednesdays of the month.

As well as having a beautiful and well maintained garden, which includes the traditional Oxfordshire game of Aunt Sally, the Killingworth Castle Inn also offers superb bed and breakfast accommodation in a recently converted stable area. Each of the four rooms is spacious and well decorated, with full en-suite facilities and the latest amenities, and, as they are separate from the pub, access is easily obtained outside of the licensing hours.

TACKLEY
MAP 3 REF D5

2½ miles NE of Woodstock off the A4260

This tranquil village, surrounded by rolling countryside, has all the features of a typical English village - pretty houses and cottages, along with the church, surrounding the central village green. Unfortunately, the manor house has long since gone but the early 17th-century gateway, an ancient dovecote, and its thatched barn can still be seen close to the village centre.

Found on the main road through Tackley, **Sturdy's Castle** is said to have been the haunt of highwaymen back in the days of stagecoach travel. Though travelling in the area is now less hazardous, this large and well laid out establishment is still offering weary travellers excellent food and drink. One of the 'Potato Pubs', visitors to Sturdy's Castle can be sure of good value for money

Sturdy's Castle, Banbury Road, Tackley, Oxon OX5 3EP
Tel: 01869 331328

and comfortable surroundings in which to enjoy the traditional atmosphere of this old inn. The bar area of open plan and it provides a lively atmosphere for those taking a glass of beer or two whilst those dining in the spacious Hole in the Wall restaurant can enjoy their meal in peace and quiet. Open all day, every day, the pub serves a delicious menu of tasty dishes which includes a mouthwatering traditional breakfast for those wishing to make an early start.

BLADON
MAP 3 REF C5

1½ miles S of Woodstock on the A4095

The village lies on the southern edge of the Blenheim estate and here, in 1965, Sir Winston Churchill was finally laid to rest in a simple grave in the churchyard. Other members of the Churchill family lie buried here including his father and mother, Randolph and Jennie, his brother John, and, his daughters. The ashes of his wife, Clementine, were interred with his grave in 1977.

As Teresa Thomas has had a life long interest in antiques, the opening and running of **Park House Tea Rooms and Antiques** combines not only her passion as a collector but also her other talents as a cook. Aided by her husband who buys and sells antiques to the American market, Teresa has made a real success of this unusual business combination. Housed in a traditional Cotswold building, the antiques are very much intertwined with the tea rooms and

Park House Tea Rooms and Antiques, 26 Park Street, Bladon, Oxon OX20 1RW Tel: 01993 812817 Fax: 01993 812912

even the tables and chairs have a price on their head. There are, also, many smaller items and, in particular, there is plenty of beautiful china, glassware, and crystal that is all clearly displayed in cabinets that have been carefully placed around the tea rooms. The sensible pricing philosophy of the antiques is extended to the delicious and mouthwatering menu. Every item is homemade, from the juicy filled sandwiches and baguettes to the luscious display of cakes and pastries. All are sure to be spoilt for choice here and Park House is certainly no place for those on a diet.

LONG HANBOROUGH
Map 3 ref C5

2 miles SW of Woodstock on the A4095

The village is home to the **Oxford Bus Museum**, the collection of an enthusiast which comprises some 40 vehicles covering public transport from 1915 to 1962. Open to the public on Sundays, the museum can also be viewed by prior arrangement.

NORTH LEIGH

MAP 3 REF C5

4 miles SW of Woodstock off the A4095

There are two main attractions to be found at North Leigh : a splendid church and a Roman villa. **St Mary's Church**, with its Saxon tower, is noted for its fine Wilcote Chapel which was built in the mid-15th century by Elizabeth Wilcote as a chantry for her two husbands and two sons.

Just to the north lies the **Roman Villa**, one of several known to have existed in this area. Built as a large country house, it had over 60 rooms, two sets of baths, an under-floor heating system, and some excellent mosaic pavements. The site is known to have been occupied by Romans from the 1st century AD, but the house, which is built around a courtyard, reached its present form in the 4th century, when it was clearly the home of a prosperous farming family and their servants. The site is open to the public from April until September.

NEW YATT

MAP 3 REF C5

4½ miles SW of Woodstock off the A4095

Found just to the west, at New Yatt, and set in the midst of the glorious Oxfordshire countryside, **The Saddlers Arms** is a charming 17th-century country inn that has undergone some modernisation. A popular place with the locals, it is not only the wonderful hospitality offered here that attracts people but also the excellent hosts and contributors to the local community, Bob Broom and Sandra Fulcher. As well as serving a superb range of beers and ales, The Saddlers Arms is also well renowned for the high quality of its food. All homemade and with a strong emphasis on fish, the menu in both the restaurant and the bar area is

The Saddlers Arms, New Yatt, near Witney, Oxon OX8 6TF
Tel: 01993 868368

well worth trying. Pub games too are played here and none are taken more seriously than Aunt Sally - the corn dolly game - for which there are competitive leagues in the county. The more usual games of darts and table skittles are also played and the local shoots are organised from the pub. Summer too sees a lot of activity at The Saddlers Arms and, in particular, the barbecue weekends are popular and well attended.

RAMSDEN
MAP 3 REF B5
5½ miles W of Woodstock off the B4022

The first mention of this village came in the mid 12th century when it was a small settlement on the edge of the **Wychwood Forest**. The village church, however, is relatively recent, it was built in 1872, although its tall bell tower is a prominent local landmark.

Found in the heart of the village, opposite the Church and War Memorial remembering the dead of the First World War, **The Royal Oak** is a charming listed coaching inn dating from the 17th century. Built of the warm and mellow Cotswold stone, the inn, which has been owned and personally run by Jon Oldham since the early 1980s, this is a popular meeting place for the locals and

The Royal Oak, Ramsden, Oxon OX7 3AU
Tel: 01993 868213

a friendly welcome is also extended to visitors who find their way here. The bar, with is low ceilings and log fires, is a delightful place for a relaxing drink at any time of the year. As a member of the CAMRA Good Beer Guide since 1991, customers also have a choice of several real ales on offer and more unusual beers from independent breweries are regularly featured here. Though the beer is certainly taken seriously here, those who prefer wine will find that there is an equally fine wine list to complement the house wines.

The Royal Oak has gained an enviable reputation for its food as well and there is a large selection of delicious home-cooked bar snacks and meals available. For those wishing to dine more formally, there is a separate small and intimate restaurant which serves an interesting and substantial menu that features the very best of local meat, fish, and vegetables. However, the excellent hospitality offered by Jon and his staff does not end there are, in the tradition an old English inn, there is also comfortable accommodation available in a choice of four en-suite guest rooms. Found in a separate building, across a pretty pave courtyard from the main inn, these bedrooms are housed in the inn's coach house and stable block. Incorporating many of the building's original features, the rooms are beautifully decorated and furnished with the modern 20th century conveniences that today's traveller has come to expect.

FINSTOCK
MAP 3 REF B5
5 miles W of Woodstock on the B4022

This charming village, which dates back to 1135, has two great literary associations. It was at the 19th-century **Holy Trinity Church**, in 1927, that TS Eliot was baptised, at the age of 38, following his controversial conversion to Catholicism. Later, the novelist, Barbara Pym, lived at Finstock for the last eight years of her life. She died in 1980 and there is a lectern in the church to her memory. Another famous resident, Sir Arthur de Cros, inventor of the pneumatic tyre, is also remembered here and his grand family mausoleum lies in the churchyard.

COMBE
MAP 3 REF C5
2 miles W of Woodstock off the A4095

This village, on the edge of the Blenheim estate, is home to the estate's sawmill. The 19th-century **Combe Mill** is occasionally opened to the public when its equipment, which includes a steam beam-engine dated 1852 and an original Cornish boiler, is set to work.

As well as once being, supposedly, home to a den of thieves, the village also had a reputation for the stupidity of its inhabitants. One story, in particular, tells how the villagers packed manure around the foundations of the church tower - to make it grow. Over night, much of the manure was washed away by heavy rain and, the next morning, a few of Combe's more gullible residents were heard to exclaim: "Look, it's grown!"

STONESFIELD
MAP 3 REF C5
3 miles W of Woodstock off the B4437

Up until the early 20th century, the village prospered from producing roofing slates, made from a Jurassic limestone that was quarried locally. At the nearby quarry a geology student discovered the fossilised remains of the earliest known stegosaurus. These were fearsome looking dinosaurs, with lashing tails armed with spikes, who lived in the area some 160 million years ago.

The name of the village, incidentally, has nothing to do with quarries or the local stone, but is derived from Stunt's or Stunta's field - Stunt being a nickname from the Old English word for foolish!

The delightful **Black Head** is a popular pub not only with the villagers but also with those taking a walk along the nearby Oxfordshire Way. At around 150 years old this is certainly not one of the oldest pubs in the area but it is sure to be one of the more lively and welcoming, particularly at weekends. Very much a drinkers pub, with four real ales and four lagers to chose from at any one time,

The Black Head, Church Street, Stonesfield, Oxon OX8 8PS
Tel: 01993 891616

there are a two comfortable bars inside. The attractive lounge bar is stylishly furnished with an open fire to add a cosy touch on a cold evening whilst the saloon bar regularly plays host to young local musicians. Customers taking advantage of the beer garden patio area can also make use of the side hatch door through which they can order their beer without leaving the garden. Owned and personally run by Simon Lane, this excellent pub also serves a good wholesome menu of pub food - of sandwiches and light snacks - and there are generally several pub games on the go including cribbage, Aunt Sally, and darts.

Found above the green in the centre of Stonesfield, **The White Horse**, like many of the buildings in the village, has a roof of local slates and what is now the function room and skittle alley was originally a barn which housed the roofing slates prior to them used in building. As well as the nine-pin skittles alley, the pub also offers customers excellent value food and drink in the same manner as the other Potato Pubs, of which this is one. With a comfortable and

The White Horse, The Ridings, Stonesfield, Oxon OX8 8EA
Tel: 01993 891604

pleasant bar area, where all can relax with a quiet drink, the inn also as an attractive and intimate dining area where the delicious menu of tasty dishes is served throughout the day. Naturally, there are potatoes on the menu in the form of an interesting and unusual list of filled jackets. As well as the choice of beers and lagers served at the bar, customers too can complement their meal with a bottle of wine from the select list that covers all tastes.

CHARLBURY
Map 3 ref B5

5 miles NW of Woodstock on the B4026

Now very much a dormitory town for Oxford, Charlbury was once famous for its glovemaking as well as being a centre of the Quaker Movement - the simple Friends' Meeting House dates from 1779 and there is also a Friends' cemetery. **Charlbury Museum**, close to the Meeting House, has displays on the traditional crafts and industries of the town and the town's charters given by Henry III and King Stephen can also be seen. Well known for its olde worlde **Railway**

Railway Station, Charlbury

Station, built by Isambard Kingdom Brunel, complete with its fishpond and hanging baskets, the town has two interesting great houses.

On the other bank of the River Evenlode from the main town lies **Cornbury Park**, a large estate that was given to Robert Dudley by Elizabeth I. Although most of the house now dates from the 17th century, this was originally a hunting lodge in Wychwood Forest that has been used since the days of Henry I. Glimpses of the house can be seen from the walk around the estate.

Lying just to the west of the town is **Ditchley Park**, a restrained and classical house built in the 1720s by James Gibbs. The interiors are splendid, having been designed by William Kent and Henry Flitcroft, and Italian craftsmen worked on the stucco decorations of the great hall and the saloon; the first treated to give an impression of rich solemnity, the second with a rather more exuberant effect.

The house has associations with Sir Winston Churchill, who used it as a weekend headquarters during World War II. Appropriately enough, given that Sir Winston had an American mother, Ditchley Park is now used as an Anglo-American conference centre.

BURFORD

Often referred to as The Gateway to the Cotswolds, Burford is an attractive old market town of honey coloured Cotswold stone found on the banks of the River Windrush. The site of a battle between the armies of Wessex and Mercia in 752, after the Norman Conquest, Burford was given to William I's brother, Bishop Odo of Bayeux. Lying on important trade routes, both north-south and east-west, the town prospered and its first market charter was granted in 1087. By the 16th century, the town was an important centre of the woollen trade and it was used as the setting for *The Woolpack*, in which the author, Celia Harknett, describes the medieval wool trade in Europe. After the decline in the wool, Burford became an important coaching centre and many of the old inns can still be seen today.

The **Church of St John the Baptist** was built on the wealth of the wool trade and this grand building has the atmosphere of a small cathedral. Originally Norman, the church has been added to over the centuries and there are several interesting monuments and plaques to be found. In the south wall of the tower stair is a caring, dated around AD 100, which shows the goddess Epona, with two male supporters whilst, the monument erected to Edmund Harman, the barber-surgeon to Henry VIII, shows North American natives - possibly the first representation of Red Indians in the country. Finally, in the south porch, is a small plaque which commemorates three Levellers who were shot in the church-yard in 1649.

The Levellers were troops from Cromwell's army who mutinied against what they saw as the drift towards the authoritarian rule they had been fighting against. While they were encamped at Burford, the Levellers were taken by surprise by Cromwell's forces. After a brief fight, some 340 prisoners were taken and placed under guard in the church. The next day there was a court martial and three of the rebels were shot as an example to the rest, who were made to watch the executions.

The town's old court house, built in the 16th century with an open ground floor and a half-timbered first floor, is now home to the **Tolsey Museum**. An interesting building in its own right, the collection on display here covers the history of the town and the surrounding area. Other buildings worth seeking out also include the 16th-century **Falkland Hall**, the home of Edmund Sylvester a local wool and cloth merchant, and **Symon Wysdom's Cottages**, which were built in 1572 by another of the town's important merchants.

Burford also has more recent literary associations as the writer Compton Mackenzie lived here before World War I. In his novel, *Guy and Pauline*, which was published in 1915, the town featured as 'Wychford'.

Situated on the original road to Witney, but now very much tucked away, **The Royal Oak** is a delightful 16th-century coaching inn that is ably run by Sue and Gary Duffy. The couple came to the pub in the late 1980s and, in the time that they have been here, they have established an enviable reputation not only for their excellent real ales but also for their food and superb standard of friendly hospitality. Known as the pub with the mugs, suspended from the ceilings in this charming old inn is a vast collection of beer mugs. The addition of a mass of old prints and photographs also helps to give The Royal Oak a homely atmosphere that is both comfortable and relaxed. Certainly a pub for those who known and enjoy a well kept pint, the food here, which is served at

The Royal Oak, Witney Street, Burford, Oxon OX18 4SN
Tel: 01993 823278

both lunchtime and in the evening, is of the same high standard. Along with the fresh homemade soups, there is also a favourite local dish that is well worth tasting - Burford Banger. However, this is not all the pub has to offer as, in the fine old tradition of an English inn, The Royal Oak has two comfortable en-suite guest rooms that are let on a bed and breakfast basis. This is the ideal place from which to explore northwest Oxfordshire and the Gateway to the Cotswolds.

AROUND BURFORD

GREAT BARRINGTON
2 miles NW of Burford off the A40

MAP 3 REF A5

Connected to its smaller neighbour, Little Barrington, by a medieval bridge over the River Windrush, this old quarry village has a pleasant church and some attractive old cottages.

To all discerning art lovers, a visit to the **Trevor Waugh Studio** is a very worth while experience. One of Britain's contemporary impressionists, many of his paintings feature on Fine Art cards and prints, Trevor has been painting since the age of four and is a graduate of the Slade School of Fine Art. Trevor's move, with his wife Michele and daughter, to the Cotswolds came in 1988 and

**Trevor Waugh Studio, Home Buildings,
Great Barrington, Burford,
Oxon OX18 4UR Tel: 01451 844781**

he found that the strong colours of the rolling countryside along with the subtlety of the Cotswold stone inspired him to paint in both oils and watercolours. Now travelling around the world, Trevor keeps a journal of paintings and sketches of his travels which not only act as inspiration when producing the larger works but are also of great interest in their own right.

The exhibition area of the Trevor Waugh Studio lies on the ground floor of a converted milking parlour - Trevor's studio is above - and, as well as the full framed works on show there are also many small unframed pictures at affordable prices. Recently Trevor has travelled extensively in the Middle East as well as journeying and exhibiting in the USA and Morocco. But perhaps he feels most at home in Italy where, not only has he made several trips since 1993, but also the sights of places such as Venice, Rome, and Florence have been the subject of exhibitions back home in the United Kingdom. With Michele looking after the business side of the gallery, Trevor is able to concentrate on his work and the studio is well worth a visit.

TAYNTON
MAP 3 REF A5
1½ miles NW of Burford off A424

Up until the end of the 19th century, this was a quarrying village, with the limestone taken from the quarries to the north being used in the construction of Blenheim Palace, most of the Oxford Colleges, Windsor Castle, and St Paul's Cathedral as well as many local buildings. The village itself is a charming huddle of stone-built thatched cottages grouped around a simple church which has a Perpendicular tower.

BLEDINGTON
MAP 3 REF A4
6 miles N of Burford on the B4450

Situated in the valley of the River Evenlode, this delightful Cotswold village has a large green and an attractive 15th-century church that is noted for its fine medieval window tracery.

Found opposite the picturesque village green **The Kings Head Inn and Restaurant** is a charming 15th-century building that has one of the most idyllic situations imaginable. A wonderful old building that has retained all its character, The Kings Head is proud of its history too and Prince Rupert of the Rhine is thought to have stayed here before the Battle of Stow in 1614. Still very much the traditional inn, visitors can enjoy a drink in the wonderful old bar, complete with the original beams, inglenook fireplace, exposed stone walls, and a

The Kings Head Inn and Restaurant, The Green, Bledington,
Oxon OX7 6XQ Tel: 01608 658365 Fax: 01608 658902
Email: kingshead@btinternet.com

warm, friendly atmosphere. There is a choice of comfortable guest rooms that not only provide visitors with all the latest 20th-century facilities but which are also furnished in a stylish manner to compliment the wonderful 15th-century surroundings.

However, The Kings Head is probably best known for the superb cuisine that is served here either in the bar or in the charming restaurant. Highly regarded locally and featured in all the best guide books, the dishes served here are lovingly prepared to order by a top team of chefs. Supplemented daily by a list of specials the mouth-watering choice is sure to please even the most jaded of palates. The restaurant also has an international wine list, that incorporates wines from lesser known vineyards, to ensure that every meal is a special occasion.

CHURCHILL
Map 3 ref B4
7½ miles N of Burford on the B4450

This quiet village has two famous sons, Warren Hastings and William Smith. Hastings, born here in a house that once stood on what is now called Hastings

Hill, went on to become the first Governor General of India in 1773. His life is as vivid as the country he administered and, following charges of corruption, he was impeached before the House of Lords. The trial dragged on for seven years and, eventually, he was personally vindicated and retired to the country at Daylesford, not far from his birthplace.

Churchill's other son, the Father of British geology, William Smith was born here in 1769. He began his professional life as a canal engineer and went on to work out the method of telling the age of geological strata by the fossils found in them. In 1815 he published a geological map of England, the first of its kind. The village's memorial to this scientific pioneer is, not surprisingly, an impressive monolith of local stone.

CORNWELL
MAP 3 REF B4
9 miles N of Burford off the A436

The village is famous as having been renovated in the 1930s by Clough William Ellis who is better known for the Italianate Welsh village of Portmeirion that he created. The 18th-century manor house did not escape Ellis' touches as he laid out the grounds.

CHASTLETON
MAP 3 REF A4
10½ miles N of Burford off the A44

This unremarkable village is home to one of the best examples of Jacobean architecture in the country. In 1602, Robert Castesby, one of the Gunpowder Plot conspirators, sold his estate here to a prosperous wool merchant from Witney, Walter Jones. A couple of years later, Jones pulled the house down and built **Chastleton House**, a splendid Jacobean manor house with a dramatic five-gabled front. Though the style suggests that the house was designed by Robert Smythson, the most famous architect of his day, there is no absolute proof of this.

Inside, the house has a wonderful collection of original panelling, furniture, tapestries, and embroideries. Of the rooms themselves, the Long Gallery, which runs the entire length of the top floor at the back of the house, is particularly impressive. This has a wonderful barrel-vaulted ceiling plastered in intricate patterns of interlacing ribbons and flowers.

OVER NORTON
MAP 3 REF B4
11 miles N of Burford off the A3400

To the northwest of the village lies the **Rollright Stones** - one of the most fascinating Bronze Age monuments in the country. These great gnarled slabs of stone stand on a ridge which offers fine views of the surrounding countryside. They also all have nicknames: the **King's Men** form a circle; the **King Stone** is to the north of the circle; and, a quarter of a miles to the west, stand the **Whis-**

Rollright Stones, Nr Over Norton

pering Knights, which are, in fact, the remnants of a megalithic tomb. Naturally, there are many local legends connected with the stones and some say that they are the petrified figures of a forgotten king and his men that were turned to stone by a witch.

SHIPTON-UNDER-WYCHWOOD   Map 3 ref B5
4 miles NE of Burford on the A361

The suffix 'under-Wychwood' derives from the ancient royal hunting forest, **Wychwood Forest**, the remains of which lie to the east of the village. The name has nothing to do with witches - wych refers to the Hwicce, a Celtic tribe of whose territory the forest originally formed a part in the 7th century. Though cleared during the Middle Ages, it was still used as a royal hunting forest until the mid-17th century. By the late 18th century there was little good wood left and the clearing of the forest was rapid to provide arable land.

The forest was one of the alleged haunts of Matthew Arnold's scholar gypsy and, in the poem, published in 1853, Arnold tells the legend of the brilliant but poor Oxford scholar who, despairing of ever making his way in the world, went to live with the gypsies to learn from their way of life.

The village itself is centred around its large green, which is dominated by the tall spire of 11th-century **St Mary's Church**. Here too can be found **The Shaven Crown**, now a hotel, which was built in the 15th century as a guest house for visitors to the nearby (and now demolished) Bruern Abbey. Finally, there is the superb **Shipton Court**, built around 1603, which is one of the country's largest Jacobean houses.

LEAFIELD
MAP 3 REF B5

4½ miles NE of Burford off the B4437

Situated on a ridge that divides the valleys of the Rivers Evenlode and Windrush, the spire of **St Michael's Church** is a local landmark that can be seen for miles around. A wholly Victorian church, it was designed by Sir George Gilbert Scott and this is his largest church in the county excluding those in Oxford.

CHIPPING NORTON
MAP 3 REF B4

10 miles NE of Burford on the A44

The highest town in Oxfordshire, at 650 feet above sea level, Chipping Norton was once an important centre of the wool trade and King John granted the town a charter to hold a fair to sell wool. Later changed to a **Mop Fair**, the tradition continues to this day when the fair is held every September.

The town's medieval prosperity can be seen in the fine and spacious **Church of St Mary** which was built in 1485 with money given by John Ashfield, a wool merchant. The splendid east window came from the Abbey of Bruern, a few miles to the southwest, which was demolished in 1535 during the Dissolution. As with many buildings in the town, there has been substantial 19th-century remodelling and the present church tower dates from 1823. However, in 1549, the minister here, the Rev Henry Joyce, was charged with high treason and hanged from the then tower because he refused to use the new prayer book introduced by Edward VI.

Still very much a market town today - the market is held on Wednesdays - Chipping Norton has been little affected by the influx of visitors who come to see this charming place. The **Chipping Norton Museum** is an excellent place to start any exploration and the permanent displays here cover local history from prehistoric and Roman times through to the present day.

Found just to the west of the town centre is **Bliss Tweed Mill**, an extraordinary sight in this area as it was designed by a Lancashire architect, George Woodhouse, in 1872 in the Versailles style. With a decorated parapet and a tall chimney which acts as a local landmark, this very northern looking mill only ceased operation in the 1980s.

Situated on the original old road between London and Stratford, **The Chequers** is a delightful 16th-century town pub. An attractive old stone-built inn, this atmospheric pub has many of its original features inside including the exposed beams, stone flagged floor and an abundance of nooks and crannies as well as real log fires in winter. The addition of a display of old photographs and prints of the town complete the picture. Kay and Josh Reid came to the pub in February 1991, and today the pub is very much a part of life in Chipping Norton. As well as the excellent range of beers, wines and lagers, The Chequers menu has an emphasis on fresh fish that is served in the superb conservatory. Kay has

**The Chequers, Gaddards Lane, Chipping Norton, Oxon OX7 5NP
Tel: 01608 644717 Fax: 01608 646237 Website: www.chequers-pub.co.uk**

spent time in Thailand at several cookery schools and the menu reflects her interest in Thai cuisine. Customers can try these wonderful fragrant dishes along with the more traditional English meals. A lovely place to stop for some rest and relaxation at any time of day, The Chequers is well worth seeking out.

MINSTER LOVELL   MAP 3 REF B5
4½ miles E of Burford off the B4047

One of the prettiest villages along the banks of the River Windrush, Minster Lovell is home to the ruins of a once impressive 15th-century manor house. **Minster Lovell Hall** was built about 1431-42 and was, in its day, one of the great aristocratic houses of Oxfordshire, the home of the Lovell family. However, one of the family was a prominent Yorkist during the Wars of the Roses and, after the defeat of Richard III at Bosworth Field, he lost his lands to the Crown.

The house was purchased by the Coke family in 1602, but around the middle of the 18th century the hall was dismantled by Thomas Coke, Earl of Leicester, and the ruins became lowly farm buildings. They were rescued from complete disintegration by the Ministry of Works in the 1930s and are now in the care of English Heritage. What is left of the house is extremely picturesque, and it is hard to imagine a better setting than here, beside the River Windrush.

One fascinating feature of the manor house which has survived is the medieval dovecote, complete with nesting boxes, which provided pigeons for the table in a way reminiscent of modern battery hen houses.

ASTHALL
Map 3 ref B5
2 miles E of Burford off the A40

This ancient hamlet lies on the route of the Roman Akeman Street at its crossing point of the River Windrush and there was certainly a Saxon river crossing here also. For such a small place, Asthall has a marvellous 12th-century church, with a unique medieval stone altar and a locally made clock tower which dates from 1665.

The Elizabethan **Manor House**, built in 1620, has a most interesting recent history. In 1919, David Freeman-Mitford, Lord Redesdale, moved into the Manor together with his wife, son, and six daughters who were later to become famous as the Mitford sisters: Nancy, Pamela, Diana, Unity, Jessica, and Deborah.

SWINBROOK
Map 3 ref B5
2 miles E of Burford off the A40

Though the great manor house of the Fettiplace family was destroyed in 1806, their impressive monuments can be seen in the parish **Church of St Mary**. However, though ornate and elaborate, the church's great feature are the two modest graves of Nancy and Unity Mitford, the sisters who grew up at nearby Asthall.

FULBROOK
Map 3 ref A5
1 mile N of Burford on the A361

Just to the northwest lies the village of Fulbrook where, situated on the main road through the village, is **The Carpenters Arms**, a delightful 16th-century inn with a traditional country feel that is owned and personally run by Lynne and John Taylor. An experienced couple, they and their friendly staff welcome both locals and those visiting the Gateway to the Cotswolds. Inside, the pub has a wonderful olde worlde atmosphere with low ceilings, open fires, and ancient timber beams and lintels. The addition of a gleaming collection of copper and brassware above the fireplaces and the old carpentry tools certainly help create a feeling of days gone by. As well as serving an excellent pint of real ale from the bar, there is also a delicious menu of tasty dishes that is sure to please everyone. Served in the dining area, which lies part in the original inn and part in a bright modern conservatory overlooking the pub garden, the mix of old

**The Carpenters Arms, Fulbrook Hill, Fulbrook, near Burford,
Oxon OX18 4BH Tel: 01993 823275**

favourites and something a little different makes eating here a real treat. A popular place for both food and drink, the traditional Sunday roast carvery is big attraction locally. Finally, during the summer, the pub's large, attractive garden comes into its own. There are swings and a climbing frame for the children who will also enjoy meeting the pet sheep and watching the birds in the aviary. Throughout the summer barbecue evenings are held regularly to which all are welcome.

8 North Oxfordshire

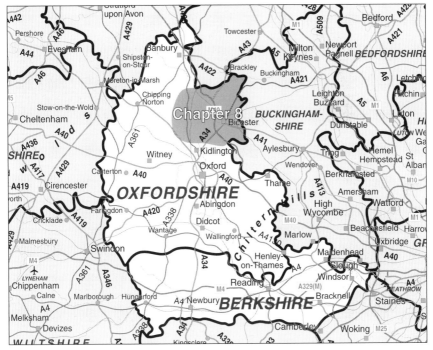

This northern region of the county, from Oxford to the Midlands, is one of rich farm land based on the clay soil. There are numerous rural villages, with ancient cottages and old stone farmhouses, that give an impression of not having changed for centuries - only the farm machinery and the television aerials give away the march of time. By far the largest town in the area is Banbury, that ancient place of the nursery rhyme and the cross. A fine blend of the old with the new, none of the town's rural heritage has been lost and today it is home to Europe's largest livestock market.

Bicester too is another ancient settlement - the Romans had a town nearby - and the settlement was first home to the Saxons. The county's most picturesque village, and some say the most delightful in the country, also lies close by. Great Tew, fortunately, was saved from complete dereliction in the 1970s and it now presents a picture of the perfect English village.

There are some fine houses to visit here also, including Sulgrave Manor, the ancestral home of George Washington, and Rousham, home to one of the few complete William Kent gardens in the country. However, lovers of rural architecture will delight in seeing Swalcliffe Barn, a magnificent 15th-century structure that is also home to a range of agricultural vehicles.

BICESTER

Though the name (which is pronounced Bister) suggests that this was a Roman settlement, the town was not, in fact, established until Saxon times and the Roman name comes as a result of the nearby and long since vanished Roman town of **Alchester**. By the time of the 12th century, the town was the home of both an Augustinian priory and also a Benedictine nunnery. Growing up around these religious houses and its market, the town suffered a disastrous fire in the early 18th century and most of the buildings seen here today date from that time onwards. Hunting and horse-racing played as much a part of the prosperity of Bicester as agriculture though industrialisation has been sporadic. The founding here of the Army's ordnance depot in 1941 has brought much new development which continued until the 1960s.

The **Church of St Eadburg** still has traces of the original 12th-century building, though over the following centuries much work on enlarging the church was undertaken. Fortunately, it is one of the few buildings which escaped the fire that wrecked the town.

Found in an attractive modern courtyard development, just behind Bicester's main shopping street, **The Stitchery** is a wonderful place to visit for anyone

The Stitchery, 18 Deans Court, Bicester, Oxon OX6 7XZ
Tel: 01869 322966

who is interested in tapestry, embroidery, and needlepoint. Owned and personally run by Carol Hill, she has turned her own interest in the crafts from a hobby into a thriving and successful business. This delightful shop is stocked full of anything and everything the keen stitcher could possibly want. There are well known starter kits for the beginner and, for the more confident, a whole range of needlework charts and tapestry canvas. Naturally, all the miscellaneous requirements are here in abundance and the shear breadth and depth of the range of coloured threads, wools, and silks that are available is mind boggling.

AROUND BICESTER

HARDWICK
MAP 3 REF E4
4 miles N of Bicester off the A43

This village of Victorian cottages is home to **Tusmore Park**, the gardens of which are open to the public on Sunday in July under the National Garden Scheme. The original fine Georgian house, built for the Fermor family, was demolished in the 1960s and replaced with a modern version.

COTTISFORD
MAP 3 REF E3
5 miles N of Bicester off the A43

This village, whose main street is some 300 yards of straight country lane, lies close to **Juniper Hill**, the birthplace of Flora Thompson, the writer who became famous for her descriptions of rural life in the late 19th century. Flora went to school in the village, a small one-storied building with a two roomed cottage at one end for the schoolmistress, which is now a private house.

MIXBURY
MAP 3 REF E3
7 miles N of Bicester off the B4031

All that remains of the Norman castle, begun in 1100, are hillocks in a nearby field though the church which they also built, in the late 12th century, is still standing. Only the south doorway of **All Saints' Church** has survived from the original building and much of the rest of the structure is the result of Victorian restoration and building work.

STRATTON AUDLEY
MAP 3 REF E4
2½ miles NE of Bicester off the A421

This small village takes its name from the position it occupied on a Roman road (Stratton) and from James Audley, a knight who fought with the Black Prince in the 14th century and was one of the first Knights of the Order of the Garter. A typical English village, the manor, Stratton House, stands opposite the **Church** of **St Mary and St Edburga,** which was built during Audley's time in the village on the site of an earlier church. The plain but elegant tower can be seen from all parts of the village.

LAUNTON
Map 3 ref E4

1½ miles E of Bicester off the A421

Now little more than a suburb of Bicester, Launton became the home of Bishop Skinner, after he was forced to leave Oxford following the Civil War. In order to spite the puritans, the Bishop is said to have ordained over 300 priests at the ancient village Church of St Mary.

MIDDLETON STONEY
Map 3 ref D4

3 miles W of Bicester on the B430

This hamlet is home to **Middleton Park**, one of the seats of the Earls of Jersey for just over 200 years. First coming here in the 1750s, the family demolished the house in the 1930s and employed Edwin Lutyens to build them a new house. This turned out to be one of the last great English country houses to be constructed but, unfortunately, the family only occupied it for eight years. Still in private hands, Middleton Park is not open to the public.

LOWER HEYFORD
Map 3 ref D4

6 miles W of Bicester on the B4030

Situated at a ford across the River Cherwell, which was replaced in the late 13th century by a stone bridge, the village lies on the opposite bank from its other half - Upper Heyford. To the south of the village lies **Rousham**, a fine house built in the mid-17th century for Sir Robert Dormer that is set in magnificent

Rousham House, Nr Lower Heyford

gardens. On the banks of the River Cherwell, the gardens were laid out by William Kent in 1738 and they represent the first phase of English landscape gardening. Fortunately little changed since it was first planted, Rousham is the only complete William Kent garden to have survived. The garden is open to the public all year round whilst the house has limited opening.

ENSTONE
MAP 3 REF C4

12 miles W of Bicester on the A44

The village's former importance as a staging post on the busy London to Worcester road can be seen in the size and number of old coaching inns. Just to the south of the village lies the **Hoar Stone**, a group of three large stones which mark the site of a prehistoric burial chamber.

MIDDLE BARTON
MAP 3 REF C4

9 miles W of Bicester on the B4030

One of the three Barton villages, Middle Barton is a collection of stone cottages and farms which have grown up around a ford across the River Dorn. To the west lies **Westcott Barton**, with its early 15th-century **Church of St Edward the Confessor**, whilst, to the southeast lies **Steeple Barton**. Here can be found **Barton Abbey**, once a cell of Osney Abbey, but which is now a private house.

Situated on the main road through Middle Barton, **The Carpenters Arms** is an attractive and striking 17th-century building that still has its thatched roof.

The Carpenters Arms, 122 North Street, Middle Barton, Oxon OX7 7DA
Tel: 01869 340378

Hard to miss, this wonderful old building is as olde worlde inside as the exterior would suggest, and the low ceilinged bar, log fires, chamber pot display, and old photographs all add to the cosy atmosphere. A comfortable place for a drink, the hosts, Adrian and June Willett, have succeeded in making this very much a home from home where all can relax. As well as the pleasant bar, there is also a separate dining area where the delicious menu of tasty dishes, which is complemented by a long list of daily specials, is served. For customers with little time on their hands the pub also offers a take away menu which includes various hot favourites from the main list. However, whilst this is a superb place for food, drink, and company, the best feature is the pub's rear beer garden. Only reached through the building, this long, peaceful garden not only has plenty of seating for customers but there are also children's swings and a climbing frame down at the bottom.

DEDDINGTON   MAP 3 REF C3
8½ miles NW of Bicester off the A423

Visitors to this old market town may find that it is familiar as this was place that was demolished by a runaway crane in the television adaptation of Tom Sharpe's *Blott on the Landscape*. The damage was, of course, cleverly faked and Deddington, which hovers between a small town and a large village, still retains all its medieval character.

Surveyed in the Domesday Book as twice the value of Banbury, the town has never developed, as Banbury and Bicester have, and it remains a prosperous agricultural centre with a still bustling market place.

Little can now be seen of the 12th-century **Deddington Castle**. This was destroyed in the 14th century and most of the building materials were put to good use in other areas of the town. However, excavations have revealed the remains of a curtain wall, a hall, and a small rectangular keep.

Meanwhile, the **Church of St Peter and St Paul** is still very visible and can be found on the edge of the Market Place. In the 1630s, the church's steeple collapsed, taking part of the main building with it and, though rebuilding work begun soon afterwards, the intervention of the Civil War made this a long project. During this time, Charles I had the church bells melted down to provide his army with another cannon. Another steeple was not built and the tower was heavily buttressed to ensure that it would never collapse.

Close by is **Castle House**, where Pier Gaveston, Edward II's favourite, was held before his execution in 1312. The house's two towers were added later, in the 1650s, when the house was in the ownership of Thomas Appletree. A supporter of Cromwell, Appletree was ordered to destroy the property of royalists and it was material from two local houses that he used in his building work.

CLIFTON   MAP 3 REF D3
8 miles NW of Bicester on the B4031

Found in the heart of Clifton, a village just to the east of Deddington, **The Duke of Cumberland's Head** is a charming old inn that offers customers the very best in hospitality. A late 16th century building of honey coloured Hornton stone and with a thatched roof, the pub was originally a row of cottages. Though many of the old features of this wonderful building can still be seen inside, there has also been some modernising work undertaken which certainly does no harm to the olde worlde atmosphere within. In the stonefaced bar area, where the exposed ceiling beams are still visible, customers can marvel at the enormous wall-mounted salmon. Caught in the 1930s by the grandfather of

**The Duke of Cumberland's Head, Clifton, near Deddington,
Oxon OX15 0PE Tel: 01869 338534**

Nick Huntington, the pub's owner, it is the biggest recorded hen salmon to have been caught in Great Britain. From the bar customers can enjoy an excellent pint of real ale from the Hook Norton brewery and, as Nick comes from Scotland, there are also over 30 malt whiskies from which to chose.

The Duke of Cumberland's Head has an equally fine reputation for the superb quality of the food served in its delightful restaurant. With an open log fire, over which there is an impressive timber lintel, the dining room is traditional, right down to the table linen and crystal glassware. Well known for the fine food, customers can enjoy a delicious menu of interesting and unusual dishes that are freshly prepared by the pub's two chefs. Finally, not only does the pub also have an attractive rear garden, with a fine lawned area and glorious displays of roses, but those looking for a place to stay will find that they have a choice of six comfortable well appointed guest rooms, each with en-suite or private bath or shower rooms.

FRITWELL
MAP 3 REF D4
5 miles NW of Bicester off the B4700

The village is home to a reputedly haunted manor house which, if the violent incidents which are said to have happened here did take place, it has every right to be. Between 1650 and 1750, a guest was killed in a duel, one brother locked his sibling in the attic as they quarrelled over a lady, and a father killed his son over a game of cards. More recent residents of the manor include Sir John Simon, a leading politician of the 1930s.

BANBURY

Famous for its cross, cakes, and the nursery rhyme, this historic and thriving market town has managed to hang on to many of its old buildings as well as become home to Europe's largest livestock market. The famous **Banbury Cross** can be found in Horsefair where it was erected, in 1859, and replaced the previous one which had been demolished by the Parliamentarians during the Civil War. Built to commemorate the marriage of Queen Victoria's oldest daughter to the Prussian Crown Prince, the figures around the bottom of the cross, of Queen Victoria, Edward VII, and George V, were added in 1914. This, obviously, is not the cross referred to in the old nursery rhyme and that cross's whereabouts is now unknown.

The town's other legendary claim to fame is its cakes, made of spicy fruit pastry, which can still be bought. Banbury was also, at one time, famous for its cheeses, which were only about an inch thick. This gave rise to the expression 'thin as a Banbury cheese'.

On the east side of the Horsefair stands **St Mary's Church**, a classical building of warm-coloured stone and hefty pillars which are pleasantly eccentric touches. The original architect was SP Cockerell, though the tower and portico were completed between 1818 and 1822 by his son, CR Cockerell. The style reflects the strong influence on English architecture of Piranesi's Views of Rome, using massive shapes and giving stone the deliberately roughened appearance which comes from the technique known as rustication.

The **Banbury Museum** also lies nearby and here can be found the story of the town's development, from the days when it came under the influence of the bishops of Lincoln, through the woollen trade of the 16th century, to the present day. The affects of the Civil War on the town were also great; the Royalists held Banbury Castle and there were two sieges here. The completion of the Coventry to Oxford Canal in 1778, the coming of the railway in 1850, and the opening of the M40 in 1991, have all played their part in making Banbury a large and successful commercial town.

Tucked away in the pedestrian precinct in the centre of Banbury, **Banesberie** is a wonderful, award winning licensed café that is well worth seeking out. The

**Banesberie, 10 Butchers Row, Banbury,
Oxon OX16 8JH Tel: 01295 269066**

name Banesberie is thought to be the original Anglo Saxon name for the town and it can be found mentioned in the Domesday Book. Owned and personally run by Tony Carney, this marvellous place is ideal for anyone who appreciates good food. Housed in a turn of the century shop, with patio seating outside and a traditional double front, the café is well decorated and comfortably furnished. With local interest prints and photographs mingling with the Art Deco prints on the walls, the style of this excellent place matches the interesting and continental flavour of the menu. From the traditional toast and tea cakes to the mouthwatering hot French and Italian-style sandwiches there is sure to be something to suit everyone here. All homecooked and with a menu that follows the seasons, it is easy to see why Banesberie has been awarded so many accolades.

**Fernleigh Guest House, 67 Oxford Road, Banbury,
Oxon OX16 9AJ Tel: 01295 250853 Fax: 269349**

Situated on the outskirts of Banbury, **Fernleigh Guest House** is an attractive large Victorian town house set back from the road. Owned and personally run by Gillian and Mark Bidwell, the couple bought the house when they returned to England from South Africa in 1997. While Mark still works as an engineer, it is Gillian, who comes from South Africa, who runs the guest house, though both are excellent cooks and they share the preparation of the delicious traditional breakfasts and the frequently changing evening dinner menu. As might be imagined, this is a spacious, three storied house which has been lovingly decorated and furnished with style and flair by the couple. The seven en-suite guest rooms are not only comfortable but Gillian has provided a number of thoughtful extras that guests will find useful. There is also a lounge and residential licensed bar. Ideal for those touring the area and popular with people on business in Banbury, Fernleigh is a warm and friendly place where guests are well looked after. The house also has ample off road parking to the rear of the premises.

AROUND BANBURY

GREAT AND LITTLE BOURTON
3 miles N of Banbury on the A423

MAP 3 REF C2

The small village of **Great Bourton**, on the western ridge of the Cherwell Valley, is home to the 13th-century All Saints Church, though much of the original building was lost when restoration work was undertaken in 1863. Cottages, built of a rich mixture of red brick and orange-brown stone, surround the churchyard.

Close by **The Plough Inn** is a charming old pub situated on the edge of the village of **Little Bourton** which overlooks the surrounding countryside. Owned

The Plough Inn, Southam Road, Little Bourton, near Banbury, Oxon OX17 1RH Tel: 01295 750222

and personally run by Andrew and Georgina Harrison, this is their first venture into the licensing trade though, as a Cordon Blue chef, Andrew has plenty of experience in catering. Attractive and welcoming inside, the comfortably furnished interior is dominated by a large open fireplace whilst the walls are adorned with a mass of old prints and photographs. Exuding olde worlde charm and hospitality, The Plough Inn is not only well known for the well kept beers, wines, and lagers that are served here but also for the superb menu of delicious food that is on offer each day. Much more than the normal run of the mill pub grub, Andrew incorporates traditional favourites whilst also including a range of flavours from around the world. Children too are welcome and with a secure beer garden to the rear, where barbecues are held in the summer, this is the ideal place to bring the whole family.

CROPREDY   MAP 3 REF C2
4 miles N of Banbury off the A423

Pronounced Cropreedy, this old heart of the village is surrounded by modern developments but is well worth finding. On the banks of the River Cherwell, with the Oxford Canal running parallel, there are terraces of old cottages and the Church of St Mary with its handsome tower. **Cropredy Bridge**, over the river, was the site of a Civil War battle, in 1644, where the Royalists defeated Cromwell's army and the church contains some relics of the conflict.

CLAYDON   MAP 3 REF C2
5½ miles N of Banbury off the A423

The most northerly village in the county, Claydon is a somewhat remote rural community with large farms coming right into the centre of the village. Here, appropriately, is the **Granary Museum of Bygones**, a fascinating place that recreates life on a farm of around a century ago. In the farm loft, there are hundreds of every day items that have long since been replaced and there are complete recreations of a cottage kitchen, a blacksmith's, and a wheelwright's workshop. In the Market Square can be found all manner of traditional shops, complete with period fittings, using old shop fronts from Banbury. A splendid way of stepping back in time, during the summer some of the old steam and traction engines are, once again, put through their paces for the public.

SULGRAVE   MAP 3 REF D2
6½ miles NE of Banbury off the B4525

This is an attractive village of thatched limestone houses and cottages and, in the village Church of St James, there is the 17th-century Washington family pew and some monuments.

Situated close to the county border with Northamptonshire and in the village of the same name, **Sulgrave Manor** is a charming small manor house that attracts many visitors during the year, particularly those from the United States. This was the ancestral home, from 1539, of the family of George Washington, the first president of the USA. Washington's family originated in the town of that name in County Durham, where their existence can be traced back to the 12th century. Moving south in the early 16th century, Lawrence Washington made a small fortune as a wool merchant in Northampton and, to put a seal on his success, purchased the Manor of Sulgrave from Henry VIII for the princely sum of £324-14s-10d!

Sulgrave Manor, Sulgrave, near Banbury, Oxon OX17 2SD
Tel: 01295 760205 Fax: 01295 768056

Great care has been taken over the years to preserve the building and its magnificent gardens so that they still give an impression of the home of a successful man of the Elizabethan times. Though, over the years, the house has been extended, the heart of the building is as Lawrence would have known it and guided tours take visitors through the various period rooms and chambers. Naturally, there are many artefacts relating to George Washington himself but there are also many items that help visitors step back in time. In particular, the kitchen has been restored to give an impression of the 250 year old room and all the utensils that would have been found there.

However, one of the most interesting and attractive features of Sulgrave Manor are the grounds. Incorporating many aspects of Elizabethan gardening there is some fine topiary work, a beautiful rose garden, a display of lavender, and some wonderful herbaceous borders. Open from March to December, visitors can also take in **The George Washington Exhibition**, The Gift Shop, and The Buttery which serves light refreshments.

MIDDLETON CHENEY
2½ miles E of Banbury on the A422

MAP 3 REF D2

This large village, which saw one of the many conflicts in this area during the Civil War, is home to a church, restored in 1865 by Sir George Gilbert Scott, which contains some splendid stained glass by Morris and Burne-Jones.

Built in the 17th century as a turnpike inn, **The New Inn** is a charming old building situated close to the road through the village. Purchased in 1998 by Tim and Jenny Kinchin, the couple have completely refurbished this wonderful old place and returned it to its former glory. With a stone flagged floor, low ceilings, and the now reinstated old brick fireplace, this is an attractive pub inside as well as outside. One unusual decorative feature are the family horse racing colours framed and mounted on the wall. Very much a family place,

**The New Inn, 45 Main Road, Middleton Cheney, Oxon OX17 2ND
Tel: 01295 710399**

children will enjoy the pet's in the garden, which include rabbits and bantam chickens, whilst they also have a play tree all to themselves. As well as serving an excellent pint of real ale, The New Inn has a fine reputation for the delicious menu of homecooked dishes that are all freshly prepared to order. Served at both lunchtime and in the evening (except Mondays and Sunday evenings), a meal here is a treat well worth taking the time to enjoy. However, this is not all this superb family pub has to offer as, most weekends, there is live music - no juke boxes here.

CHACOMBE

2½ miles NE of Banbury of the A422

Map 3 ref D2

Just to the north, in the heart of the quiet village of Chacombe, lies **The George and Dragon**, a charming 16th-century inn that acts as a popular meeting place for the people of Chacombe and the surrounding area. A warm and welcoming place, thanks to the owner and landlord, Ray Bennett, this attractive pub offers the very best in hospitality in a relaxed and easy style. As can be expected with a building of this age, the ceilings are low and the cosy restaurant still has the original stone flagged floor. However, not many buildings dating from the 1700s

The George and Dragon, Silver Street, Chacombe, near Banbury, Oxon OX17 2JR Tel: 01295 711500

can boast that they retain one of their original doors but here can be seen, giving access to the main bar from the rear of the pub, The George and Dragon's original massive wooden door. An excellent place to come to for a quiet drink, the pub is also fast gaining an enviable reputation for the superb meals that are on offer. Served in either the bar or the restaurant, Ray's two young and imaginative chefs have added their unique style and flair to some well loved favourites as well as incorporating a wide range of tastes in their constantly changing blackboard menu. Finally, accommodation too is available at The George and Dragon. The two en-suite guest rooms are both furnished and decorated to the very highest standards and whilst one is interestingly located in the roof of the building the other has a Breton style box bed.

ADDERBURY
MAP 3 REF D3
3 miles SE of Banbury off the A4260

The village is actually separated into two halves, West and East Adderbury, by a brook though, today, they are often referred to as one. The key feature of interest here is **Adderbury House**, a dark ironstone building, constructed in 1624, which was the home of John Wilmot, 2nd Earl of Rochester, after his marriage to Elizabeth Malet in 1667. However, Wilmot spent little time here, preferring to spend his time at the court of Charles II. A well known wit, poet, and rake, Wilmot managed to scandalise even the easy going king and he died, in 1680, at the age of 33 - some say he was worn out by sensual pleasure.

Later inhabitants have included two Scottish dukes and the owner of a horse which won the Derby at 100 to 1 in the 19th century. It is now a rather sad building as much of it was subsequently demolished.

Situated on the village green, **The Red Lion Hotel** has a history that is as interesting as Adderbury's itself. Dating from the 16th century, during restoration work in one of the bedrooms, the royal arms of Henry VIII surmounting those of the Bustard family, were found beneath layers of lath and plaster. This

The Red Lion Hotel, The Green, Adderbury, Oxon OX17 3LU
Tel: 01295 810269

would suggest that the hostelry was, at one time, called with the Royal Arms or the King's Head. However, the inn gained it present name during the Civil War when there were many skirmishes between the Royalists and the Parliamentarians in the village and surrounding area. In fact, local folk lore has it that the secret tunnel found in the inn's wine vaults was an intended escape route for the Cavaliers should the Roundheads lay siege.

The inn's subsequent history is less colourful and it has followed the lines of many such places by first becoming a coaching inn and now a delightful country hotel. The oldest inn in Adderbury, this attractive honey coloured stone building has been beautifully restored and luxuriously decorated whilst also ensuring that the original features, such as the ancient oak beams and large stone fireplaces, are seen at their best. Owned and personally run by Susie and Steve Drysdale, The Red Lion has plenty to offer its guests. There are 12 charming en-suite guest rooms, which combine all the modern conveniences expected by today's traveller with an elegance of yesteryear. Each has been individually designed and furnished to suit the character of each of the rooms.

As well as the cosy and attractive traditional country drawing room, guests will find that there are two equally comfortable bars from which they can enjoy a wide variety of real ales and fine wines. However, it is perhaps for its restaurant that The Red Lion is best known locally. Offering the very best in both English and Continental cuisine, a meal in this characterful restaurant is a treat well worth savouring. Finally, one last feature of the hotel that is worthy of a mention is the inn's old well. Now glazed over for safety reasons, the movement of the natural spring water, 47 feet below, can be detected and the well was used back in the days when the inn produced its own ale.

SOUTH NEWINGTON   MAP 3 REF C3
6 miles SW of Banbury on the A361

This small village, built almost entirely of ironstone, is home to the fine **Church of St Peter Ad Vincula**. Inside can be found some of the county's best medieval wall paintings which were created around 1330. What makes these paintings so special is the detail of the figures: Thomas à Becket, the martyrdom of Thomas of Lancaster, and St Margaret slaying a dragon.

GREAT TEW   MAP 3 REF C4
7½ miles SW of Banbury off the B4022

One of the most picturesque villages in Oxfordshire, if not in England, it is amazing that Great Tew has survived. In 1978, this planned estate village had fallen into such a state of disrepair that, in order to save it, Great Tew was declared a conservation area. Today, the 16th, 17th and 18th-century thatched cottages and houses nestle in a fold in the landscape of rolling countryside.

The village looks so much a natural part of the landscape now that it is interesting to learn that it was deliberately made to look more picturesque in the early 19th century. At this time villages were often demolished by the landowners to whom they belonged, so as not to spoil the view from the great house, but here the cottages were improved and trees planted in order to ensure the required vista.

The house in this case was **Great Tew Park**, on rising ground to the south of the village, and the present house is mostly 19th century, although the stables are earlier, about 1700. However, its 17th-century predecessor, the home of Lucius Carey, Lord Falkland, was a gathering place for the intellectuals of the day, including the authors Abraham Cowley, Edmund Waller, and Ben Jonson and scholars from Oxford. Of this house only the garden walls remain.

The beautiful half-thatched, half-tiled **Falkland Arms** dates back to the 16th century and it remains one of the country's last unspoilt true English pubs. Once owned by the Falkland family - the 5th Viscount in the 17th century was secretary to the Navy and he gave his name to the Falkland Islands - this traditional country inn has changed little since then. The bar, with its heavy oak

The Falkland Arms, Great Tew, Chipping Norton, Oxon OX7 4DB
Tel: 01608 683653

beams, flagstone floor, and large inglenook fireplace, is as welcoming today as it has been to travellers over the centuries and not only is there a fine selection of beers and real ales here but the inn is also well known for its range of English country wines and ciders. The interesting and unusual collection of over 300 ceramic drinking mugs hanging from the ceiling beams only adds to the atmosphere.

Managed by Anne and Tim Newman, in the short time that this energetic and friendly couple have been here, they have certainly turned around the fortunes of the pub and made it one of the best inns in the area. Whilst Tim is looking after patrons in the bar, Anne is busy ensuring that the delicious and interesting menu served at both lunchtime and in the evening (except Sundays) is equal to the high standards set by the rest of the hospitality at The Falkland Arms. The dining room itself is only tiny so booking is essential and, as the menu changes daily, those staying here will certainly not tire of the choice. Finally, in the true tradition of a real English inn, accommodation, in six beautifully decorated and furnished en-suite guest rooms is available. Breakfast is served at the civilised hour of 09.00 and, to ensure that guests have a real away from it all break, children under 14 years and pets are not allowed here.

SWERFORD   MAP 3 REF C3
7 miles SW of Banbury off the A361

Lying deep in the valley of the River Swere, the village is home to the **St Mary's Church** which has architectural features from the 13th, 14th, and 15th centuries as well as some fascinating exterior gargoyles. Behind the church can be found, in the mounds and earthworks, evidence of an old castle.

With stunning views over the Swere Valley, **The Masons Arms** is a delightful country inn that is owned and personally run by Linda and Trevon. With a philosophy of *"set out of town, but still in the High Street"*, this charming place is a happy mix of relaxed style with excellent service. Dating back over approximately 200 years, this charming old building has been well looked after over the years and today it is a comfortable place with a warm and welcoming decor. As Trevon has been a family butcher, it is not surprising to see a set of butchers weights and scales on display in the pub. From the bar a range of well kept traditional ales from an award winning local brewery are served. Food, too, is very important here and an excellent menu of delicious homemade meals are prepared by the pub's chef. Served in the cosy and separate restaurant, a meal here is a treat well worth trying. Those looking for less formal dining may like to try the more traditional menu of pub meals served in the bar area. As this is

The Masons Arms, Swerford, near Chipping Norton, Oxon OX7 4AP
Tel: 01608 683212

a true inn, accommodation in the form of three en-suite guest rooms is available, which all come up to the same high standard as the rest of this superb inn. Easy to reach and well located for the attractions of north Oxfordshire, The Masons Arms is an ideal place for all the family and the children, particularly, will enjoy their purpose built play area as well as watching the birds in the aviary. The Masons Arms has been modernised in the last few years and has excellent disabled facilities. Groups are already using the pub on tour for day excursions.

HOOK NORTON
MAP 3 REF B3
7 miles SW of Banbury off the A361

This large village is famous for being the home of one of the few remaining family-run breweries. Hook Norton Brewery was set up by John Harris from his farmhouse in 1849, where he started as a malster in the farm's malthouse. One thing led to another and, after some experimentation, Harris constructed a purpose built brewery in 1872. Though John died in 1887, the brewery, which moved to its present premises in 1900, has continued to stay in the family and it remains a local brewery with around 35 tied pubs in the immediate area.

The Pear Tree Inn is a large, attractive brick built pub, in the heart of the village, that dates back to the 1800s. Managed since 1997 by Carol and John Sivyer, this warm and friendly place attracts not only the local people but those from far and wide - the pub appears in various guide books. As well as offering an excellent range of real ales, including local brews, this is also an superb place to come to for wholesome bar snacks and meals that just stop short of a three course meal. Along with the traditional favourites, the Hookey casserole is a popular treat that is well worth coming to try. Those looking for overnight

The Pear Tree Inn, Scotland End, Hook Norton, near Banbury, Oxon OX15 5NU Tel: 01608 737482

accommodation will also find that The Pear Tree Inn will meet their needs very well. There are two comfortable en-suite guest rooms at the inn that are both of an exceptional size and they too are well furnished and decorated.

However, it is the special events which John organises that makes The Pear Tree Inn so special. Morris dancers provide an unusual diversion during the summer whilst there is also an annual beer festival and various regular music events. Perhaps though the most interesting are the evenings that are arranged to coincide with the first and last Grand Prix of the season. Always well attended, the events run through the night due to the location of the motor racing and the night is rounded off with a splendid salmon and champagne breakfast.

BLOXHAM   MAP 3 REF C3
3½ miles SW of Banbury on the A361

Dominated by the 14th-century St Mary's Church, whose spire is a highly visible local landmark and its Victorian public school, this large village is one of narrow lanes and fine gentlemen's houses. The old court house, to the south of the church, contains the **Bloxham Village Museum**, where there is a permanent collection of items on display which tell the life of the inhabitants of the village and surrounding area.

BROUGHTON   MAP 3 REF C3
2½ miles SW of Banbury on the B4035

The moated mansion, **Broughton Castle**, was built in 1300 by Sir John de Broughton as his manor on the site of the existing house. Extended and altered in the 16th century to turn it into a fine Tudor home, the house has been owned by the same family since 1451. Over the years, there have been several Royal visitors including Queen Anne of Denmark, wife of James I. Both James I

Broughton Castle, Broughton

and Edward VII have used the aptly named King's Chamber, with its handpainted Chinese wall paper. The house also played a part in the Civil War as it has a secret room where leaders of the Parliamentary forces laid their plans.

Situated just to the north, at **North Newington**, on the Broughton Castle estate, **Broughton Grounds Farm** has been worked by Andrew and Margaret Taylor's family for three generations since 1914. Still a working mixed farm of 250 acres, from the large 17th-century honey coloured stone built farmhouse, Margaret offers superb bed and breakfast accommodation in a choice of two comfortable colour coordinated guest rooms. A typical large and spacious farmhouse, with glorious views over the surrounding countryside, this is a warm and friendly place to stay. Genuine free range eggs are on the menu for breakfast and the chickens can be seen out in the fields so guests know just how fresh

Broughton Grounds Farm, North Newington, near Banbury, Oxon OX15 6AW Tel: 01295 730315

they are; in fact, one of Margaret's customers travels 20 miles just for the eggs! Guests can enjoy the peace and quiet of the garden, or take a walk in the beautiful countryside. Broughton Grounds Farm is a delightful place to stay and children particularly will enjoy seeing a working farm at close quarters.

SWALCLIFFE
Map 3 ref C3
5 miles W of Banbury on the B4035

The village is dominated by the large **Church of St Peter and St Paul** which towers over all the other buildings here. Founded in Saxon times, the bulk of the building dates from the 12th, 13th, and 14th centuries and it is the tracery in the east window which makes the church noteworthy.

However, by far the most impressive building in Swalcliffe is the **Barn**, which has been acknowledged as one of the finest 15th-century half-cruck barns in the country. Built as the manorial barn by New College, Oxford, in 1400-1409, it was used to store produce from the manor and never to store tithes. Today, it is home to a collection of agricultural and trade vehicles.

Swalcliffe Church

To the northeast of the village, on **Madmarston Hill**, are the remains of an Iron Age hill fort which was occupied from the 2nd century BC to the 1st century AD.

Situated on the opposite side of the village green from the church, **The Stag's Head** is a wonderful old thatched roof pub that dates from the 15th century. Owned by David and Pam Morgan, this is a traditional village pub offering a warm welcome to all. In fact it is David and Pam's proud boast that canine friends are particularly welcome provided they can keep their owners under control! As might be expected with a building of this age, there are many interesting features inside and apart from the low ceilings and the exposed beams, there is a wonderful inglenook fireplace complete with its original spice box. Throughout this cosy and comfortable pub there is also a large collection of pots, jugs, and other domestic ceramic items either hanging from the ceiling or displayed elsewhere. As well as offering real ales, The Stag's Head has a range of eight wines, red and white, all of which are sold either by the glass or by the bottle. Food too is an important part of the life of the pub and the interesting bar meals and evening menu

The Stag's Head, The Green, Swalcliffe, Oxon OX15 5EJ Tel: 01295 780232

of tasty dishes, served every session except Sunday evenings and Mondays, make it well worth seeking out. During the summer, the glorious four terrace garden really comes into its own and there is plenty of seating so that customers can enjoy the peace of this mature, well tendered garden. Children too are taken care of and there is a purpose built play area for them also out in the garden.

Situated on a hill overlooking the village of Swalcliffe, **Partway House** is the delightful home of Erica and Malcolm Brown. Originally built as a lodge in 1947, this attractive honey coloured stone building was bought by the couple in 1977 and, following some extensive work on the house, which includes a tasteful extension, they took up residence in 1984. From this superb, spacious property, the couple offer wonderful bed and breakfast accommodation in a choice of three comfortable, well decorated, and furnished guest rooms. After enjoying a peaceful night's sleep, guests can enjoy a delicious breakfast in another delightful room and there is also a charming guest lounge, complete with real fire. A superb dinner, and Sunday lunch, are available by prior arrange-

Partway House, Swalcliffe, near Banbury, Oxon OX15 5HA
Tel: 01295 780246

ment. Though the house is beautifully presented, with style and flair, it is perhaps the garden, over which all the bedrooms look, that is Partway House's most attractive feature. Sited on one of the highest points in Oxfordshire, the large, mature garden contains many unusual plants that have been supplied by their son's specialist nursery. There are glorious views over uninterrupted countryside at the end of a long herbaceous walk, with shrub and rhododendron borders, roses, and an excellent kitchen garden. Partway House is open to guests throughout the year, except Christmas and New Year.

BRAILES
MAP 3 REF B3
9 miles W of Banbury on the B4035

Just to the north of the village lies **Compton Wynyates**, the famous Tudor mansion of the Marquis of Northampton. Of brick and timber and built around a courtyard, the house is unfortunately not open to the public.

Found in the heart of rural Oxfordshire and part of the Compton Wynyates estate, **Agdon Farm** is a working beef, sheep, and arable farm that has been managed by Richard and Maggie Cripps for over 30 years. At the centre of the farm is the large 18th-century farmhouse from which that are stunning views

Agdon Farm, Brailes, near Banbury, Oxon OX15 5JJ
Tel: 01608 685226

over the rolling countryside in all directions. From the house Maggie and Richard offer excellent bed and breakfast accommodation in a choice of three superb and well appointed guest rooms. Ideal for discerning visitors seeking peace and tranquillity, this warm and friendly house is a place well worth finding. As well as the well furnished and decorated guest rooms, those fortunate enough to stay here also have the use of a television lounge, complete with a cosy open fire, and the substantial homecooked traditional breakfast, and evening meals if requested, are served in an equally comfortable dining room. Guests here are very much one of the family and the whole house has those finishing touches, such as antique furniture and family photographs, that make it a real home from home. The exterior of the wonderful stone house is equally impressive and the mature garden includes a well used vegetable garden that helps to keep the dining table full.

WROXTON   Map 3 ref C2
3 miles NW of Banbury on the A422

This charming village of local brown stone cottages cluster around the village duckpond from which a road leads to the entrance of **Wroxton Abbey**. This impressive Jacobean mansion was built by the Earl of Downe and it remained in the North family for 300 years. Frederick, Lord North, was prime minister at the time that England lost the American War of Independence and, ironically, the abbey today is owned by a New Jersey university. The gardens and grounds of the abbey, restored as an 18th-century park, are open to the public though the house is not.

TOURIST INFORMATION CENTRES

Locations in **bold** type are open throughout the year

Berkshire

Aldermaston Tourist Information Centre
Aldermaston Wharf, Padworth, Reading, Berkshire, RG7 4JS
Tel No: 0118 971 2868

Bracknell Tourist Information Centre
The Look Out, Nine Mile Ride, Bracknell, Berkshire, RG12 7QW
Tel No: 01344 868196

Maidenhead Tourist Information Centre
The Library, St Ives Road, Maidenhead, Berkshire, SL6 1QU
Tel No: 01628 781110

Newbury Tourist Information Centre
The Wharf, Newbury, Berkshire, RG14 5AS
Tel No: 01635 30267

Reading Tourist Information Centre
Town Hall, Blagrave Street, Reading, Berkshire, RG1 1QH
Tel No: 0118 956 6266

Windsor Tourist Information Centre
24 High Street, Tel No: Windsor, Berkshire, SL4 1LH
Tel No: 01753 743900

Wokingham Tourist Information Centre
The Town Hall, Market Place, Wokingham, Berkshire, RG40 1AS
Tel No: 0118 977 4772

Oxfordshire

Abingdon Tourist Information Centre
25 Bridge Street, Abingdon, Oxfordshire, OX14 3HN
Tel No: 01235 522711

Banbury Tourist Information Centre
Banbury Museum, 8 Horsefair, Banbury, Oxfordshire, OX16 0AA
Tel No: 01295 259855

Bicester Tourist Information Centre
Unit 6A, Bicester Village, Pingle Drive, Bicester, Oxfordshire, OX6 7WD
Tel No: 01869 369055

Burford Tourist Information Centre
The Brewery, Sheep Street, Burford, Oxfordshire, OX18 4LP
Tel No: 01993 823558

Cherwell Valley Tourist Information Centre
Motorway Service Area J10/M40, Northampton Road, Ardley, Bicester,
Oxfordshire, OX6 9RD Tel No: 01869 345888

Chipping Norton Tourist Information Centre
The Guildhall, Chipping Norton, Oxfordshire, OX7 5NJ
Tel No: 01608 644379

Didcot Tourist Information Centre
The Car Park, Station Road, Didcot, Oxfordshire, OX11 7AU
Tel No: 01235 813243

Faringdon Tourist Information Centre
7A Market Place, Faringdon, Oxfordshire, SN7 7HL
Tel No: 01367 242191

Henley-on-Thames Tourist Information Centre
Town Hall, Market Place, Henley-on-Thames, Oxfordshire, RG9 2AQ
Tel No: 01491 578034

Oxford Tourist Information Centre
The Old School, Gloucester Green, Oxford, Oxfordshire, OX1 2DA
Tel No: 01865 726871

Thame Tourist Information Centre
Market House, North Street, Thame, Oxfordshire, OX9 3HH
Tel No: 01844 212834

Wallingford Tourist Information Centre
Town Hall, Market Place, Wallingford, Oxfordshire, OX10 0EG
Tel No: 01491 826972

Wantage Tourist Information Centre
Vale and Downland Museum, 19 Church Street, Wantage,
Oxfordshire, OX12 8BL Tel No: 01235 760176

Witney Tourist Information Centre
Town Hall, 51A Market Square, Witney, Oxfordshire, OX8 6AG
Tel No: 01993 775802

Woodstock Tourist Information Centre
Hensington Road, Woodstock, Oxfordshire, OX20 1JQ
Tel No: 01993 811038

INDEX OF TOWNS, VILLAGES AND PLACES OF INTEREST

INDEX OF PLACES TO STAY, EAT, DRINK & SHOP

THE HIDDEN PLACES ORDER FORM

To order any of our publications just fill in the payment details below and complete the order form **overleaf**. For orders of less than 4 copies please add £1 per book for postage and packing. Orders over 4 copies are P & P free.

Please Complete Either:

I enclose a cheque for £ .... made payable to Travel Publishing Ltd

Or:

Card No:

Expiry Date:

Signature: ....

NAME: ....

ADDRESS: ....

....

....

POSTCODE: ....

TEL NO: ....

Please send to: Travel Publishing Ltd
7a Apollo House
Calleva Park
Aldermaston
Berks, RG7 8TN

THE HIDDEN PLACES
ORDER FORM

	Price	Quantity	Value
Regional Titles			
Cambridgeshire & Lincolnshire	£7.99	....	....
Channel Islands	£6.99	....	....
Cheshire	£7.99	....	....
Chilterns	£7.99	....	....
Cornwall	£7.99	....	....
Devon	£7.99	....	....
Dorset, Hants & Isle of Wight	£7.99	....	....
Essex	£7.99	....	....
Gloucestershire	£6.99	....	....
Heart of England	£4.95	....	....
Hereford, Worcs & Shropshire	£7.99	....	....
Highlands & Islands	£7.99	....	....
Kent	£7.99	....	....
Lake District & Cumbria	£7.99	....	....
Lancashire	£7.99	....	....
Norfolk	£7.99	....	....
Northeast Yorkshire	£6.99	....	....
Northumberland & Durham	£6.99	....	....
North Wales	£7.99	....	....
Nottinghamshire	£6.99	....	....
Peak District	£6.99	....	....
Potteries	£6.99	....	....
Somerset	£6.99	....	....
South Wales	£7.99	....	....
Suffolk	£7.99	....	....
Surrey	£6.99	....	....
Sussex	£6.99	....	....
Thames Valley	£7.99	....	....
Warwickshire & West Midlands	£6.99	....	....
Wiltshire	£6.99	....	....
Yorkshire Dales	£6.99	....	....
Set of any 5 Regional titles	**£25.00**	....	....
National Titles			
England	£9.99	....	....
Ireland	£9.99	....	....
Scotland	£9.99	....	....
Wales	£8.99	....	....
Set of all 4 National titles	**£28.00**	....	....

For orders of less than 4 copies please add £1 per book for postage & packing. Orders over 4 copies P & P free.

THE HIDDEN PLACES
READER COMMENT FORM

The *Hidden Places* research team would like to receive reader's comments on any visitor attractions or places reviewed in the book and also recommendations for suitable entries to be included in the next edition. This will help ensure that the *Hidden Places* series continues to provide its readers with useful information on the more interesting, unusual or unique features of each attraction or place ensuring that their stay in the local area is an enjoyable and stimulating experience.

To provide your comments or recommendations would you please complete the forms below and overleaf as indicated and send to: The Research Department, Travel Publishing Ltd., 7a Apollo House, Calleva Park, Aldermaston, Reading, RG7 8TN.

Your Name:

Your Address:

Your Telephone Number:

Please tick as appropriate: Comments ☐   Recommendation ☐

Name of *"Hidden Place"*:

Address:

Telephone Number:

Name of Contact:

THE HIDDEN PLACES
READER COMMENT FORM

Comment or Reason for Recommendation:

....

....

....

....

....

....

....

....

....

....

....

....

THE HIDDEN PLACES
READER COMMENT FORM

The *Hidden Places* research team would like to receive reader's comments on any visitor attractions or places reviewed in the book and also recommendations for suitable entries to be included in the next edition. This will help ensure that the *Hidden Places* series continues to provide its readers with useful information on the more interesting, unusual or unique features of each attraction or place ensuring that their stay in the local area is an enjoyable and stimulating experience.

To provide your comments or recommendations would you please complete the forms below and overleaf as indicated and send to: The Research Department, Travel Publishing Ltd., 7a Apollo House, Calleva Park, Aldermaston, Reading, RG7 8TN.

Your Name:

Your Address:

Your Telephone Number:

Please tick as appropriate: Comments ☐   Recommendation ☐

Name of *"Hidden Place"*:

Address:

Telephone Number:

Name of Contact:

THE HIDDEN PLACES
READER COMMENT FORM

Comment or Reason for Recommendation:

....

....

....

....

....

....

....

....

....

....

....

....

....

THE HIDDEN PLACES
READER COMMENT FORM

The *Hidden Places* research team would like to receive reader's comments on any visitor attractions or places reviewed in the book and also recommendations for suitable entries to be included in the next edition. This will help ensure that the *Hidden Places* series continues to provide its readers with useful information on the more interesting, unusual or unique features of each attraction or place ensuring that their stay in the local area is an enjoyable and stimulating experience.

To provide your comments or recommendations would you please complete the forms below and overleaf as indicated and send to: The Research Department, Travel Publishing Ltd., 7a Apollo House, Calleva Park, Aldermaston, Reading, RG7 8TN.

Your Name:

Your Address:

Your Telephone Number:

Please tick as appropriate: Comments ☐   Recommendation ☐

Name of *"Hidden Place"*:

Address:

Telephone Number:

Name of Contact:

THE HIDDEN PLACES
READER COMMENT FORM

Comment or Reason for Recommendation:

....

....

....

....

....

....

....

....

....

....

....

....

THE HIDDEN PLACES
READER COMMENT FORM

The *Hidden Places* research team would like to receive reader's comments on any visitor attractions or places reviewed in the book and also recommendations for suitable entries to be included in the next edition. This will help ensure that the *Hidden Places* series continues to provide its readers with useful information on the more interesting, unusual or unique features of each attraction or place ensuring that their stay in the local area is an enjoyable and stimulating experience.

To provide your comments or recommendations would you please complete the forms below and overleaf as indicated and send to: The Research Department, Travel Publishing Ltd., 7a Apollo House, Calleva Park, Aldermaston, Reading, RG7 8TN.

Your Name:

Your Address:

Your Telephone Number:

Please tick as appropriate: Comments ☐   Recommendation ☐

Name of *"Hidden Place"*:

Address:

Telephone Number:

Name of Contact:

THE HIDDEN PLACES
READER COMMENT FORM

Comment or Reason for Recommendation:

....

....

....

....

....

....

....

....

....

....

....

....

MAP SECTION

The following pages of maps encompass the main cities, towns and geographical features of the Thames Valley, as well as many of the interesting places featured in the guide. Distances are indicated by the use of scale bars located below each of the maps

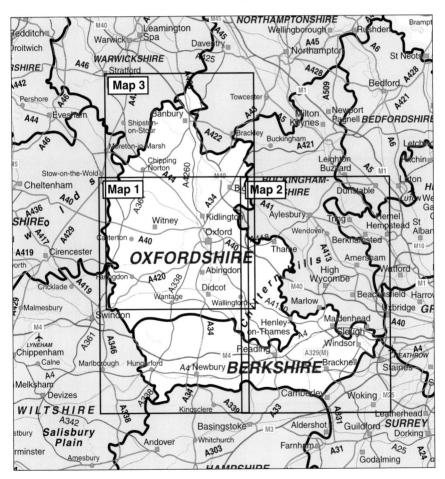

Map 1

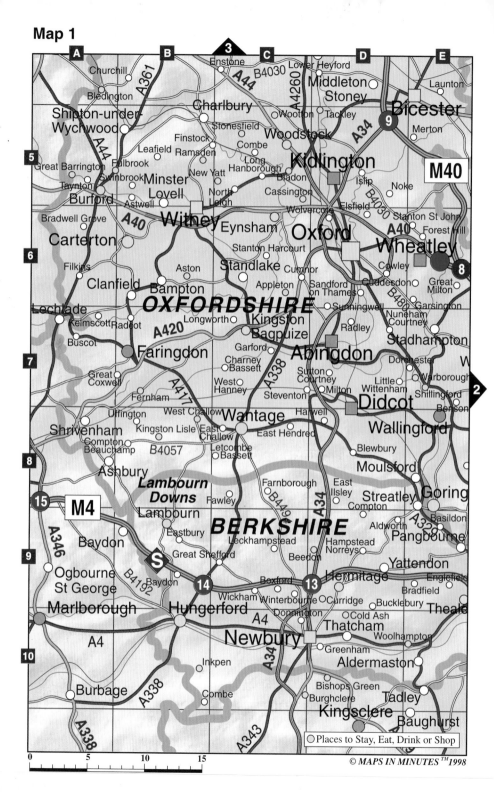

© *MAPS IN MINUTES* ™1998

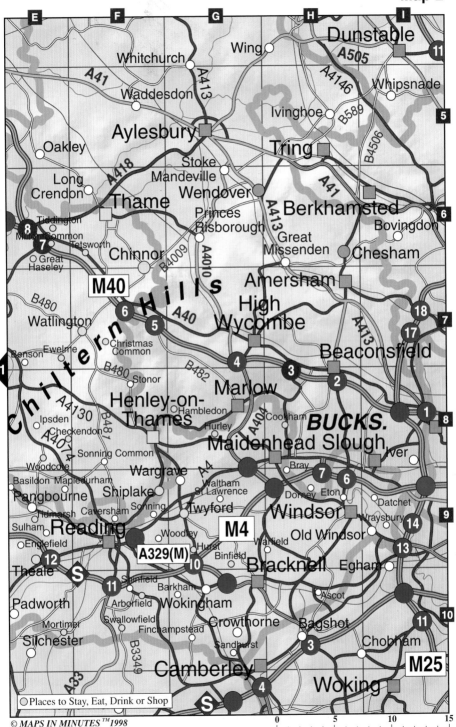

Map 2

Map 3

© MAPS IN MINUTES ™ 1998

Places to Stay, Eat, Drink or Shop